The Smile on the Face of the Pig

The Smile on the Face of the Pig
Confessions of the Last Cub Reporter

John Bull

CHAPLIN BOOKS

www.chaplinbooks.co.uk

First published in 2011 by Chaplin Books
Copyright © John Bull

ISBN 978-0-9565595-4-8

A CIP catalogue record for this book is available
from The British Library.

Design by 131 Design
Printed in the UK by Ashford Colour Press

Chaplin Books
1 Eliza Place
Gosport PO12 4UN
Tel: 023 9252 9020
www.chaplinbooks.co.uk

For many years this engraving, from an original drawing by WH Snape, hung in the general manager's room of the *Portsmouth Evening News*

'The past is a foreign country: they do things differently there.'
L.P. Hartley

'Be kind to me. I was born on a younger planet than this one.'
John Bull

CHAPTERS

ACKNOWLEDGEMENTS

Thanks to those at the *News*, past and present, Debbie Croker, Ian Plowman, Roy West and Graham Hewitt, and all those reporters whose ideas I pinched: Peter Michel, Trevor Fishlock, Alan Biggs and Phil Griffiths. Thanks also to David Trenbirth; Michael Heaps of Kingswell, Berney, Mangnall and Heaps; Patrick Miller; my editor Amanda Field; Bay House School; and Miss Fenella Fielding.

(There are many others – but who would want to follow Fenella?)

Before the mouth took on a cynical twist: me at age 17

Chapter One
The Great Freeze

The first flakes came spinning out of the January night sky as our family took the ferry home to Gosport from the panto *Cinderella* at the Kings Theatre, Southsea. I wanted to stay on deck to watch the magic crystals fall from the sky. Gosport never used to get more than a dusting of snow and, being an 11-year-old schoolboy, I didn't want to miss any of it. I needn't have worried. That bitter winter of 1947 we had more than enough to satisfy even the most romantic kid.

My father said that the wind that howled for weeks on end came straight from the Urals in Russia. Some parts of the country suffered terribly: it was a blow that Mr Attlee's government, struggling to get the country on its feet again after the devastation of war, probably didn't deserve. Our teachers talked about factories working only part-time, the railways grinding to a halt. There wasn't enough food or coal. Many people died before their time – vulnerable babies, the elderly and the sick.

The first blizzard left snowdrifts such as few Gosport folk had ever seen; before they could be cleared, more came, snow on snow. Most pavements had a wall of dirty, black ice piled up from attempts to clear it. We had days when the snow seemed to thaw, only for the night to freeze everything again. Apart from the well-used bus routes, cars and lorries had to drive in the tracks left by others. There were still a lot of horse-drawn deliveries then. We felt sorry for the horses, shivering under their blankets. In our road, Queen's Road, I remember neighbours struggling to free the coalman's mare when she slipped and fell, tangled up in the harness.

My mother went about padded up: two cardigans under her coat and a scarf permanently tied round her head and face. Even glamorous Elsie, the likely miss from the next street, began to look like a Russian grandmother. The lady next door was seen in the garden one day chopping up the kitchen table to burn on the fire. My father, who always prided himself on being well-shod, had the bright idea of burning old shoes. They actually did offer a surprising amount of warmth. We shared this discovery with family and neighbours and by the time the long, long prayed-for thaw came in March, I don't suppose there was an old pair of boots left in the town.

For most of us kids it was a delicious 'time out of time'. The old town was surrounded by a defensive moat and that, of course, was frozen solid. Boys and girls walked about on it, treating it like a country lane. It gave us a unique opportunity to go places without bothering to ask – like St George's barracks. All we had to do was slither down the bank behind the burnt-out shell of the Ritz cinema and walk under the bridge in Walpole Road, by-passing all fences, gates and guards.

For a change we'd go the other way along the moat: apart from a detour where the town fathers had thoughtlessly placed the swimming pool, we could walk on the ice all the way to where the sluices fed the moat from the harbour and Haslar creek. I'd stand with my friends under the little road bridge by Holy Trinity Church, eavesdropping on the conversations of passers-by above, mostly submarine sailors from HMS Dolphin. Very educational that was. We made a toboggan from a soap-box, and fitted it with hardwood runners. This we took to the high, sloping ramparts behind Canon Barclay's Holy Trinity vicarage. It was a satisfying Cresta Run, and at the bottom, if you didn't overturn, you shot straight out onto the ice.

Most locals wouldn't have said that Gosport in 1947 was attractive, and the dirty snow and slush on the streets did not add much charm. Though in the open, looking out over the harbour to Pompey, we were treated to vistas of white solitude framed by a sky of black ink – very dramatic, very romantic. From Ann's Hill, the highest point in Gosport (actually an arch over Queen Victoria's old Gosport-to-Fareham railway line with an altitude of 21ft-ish), look to the east and you'll see ... nothing. Because there is nothing. The view over Portsmouth Harbour goes on across the eastern flatlands of England, the North Sea, the north German plain, the plains of Poland, the empty, endless *versts* of Russia to the next highest point, the stark mountains of the Urals. The coldest place. At least that's what one of my teachers once told us. But then, he was a dreamer. *"Où sont les neiges d'antan?"* asked that earlier romantic poet François Villon. That's where the snows of yesteryear pile up: take my teacher's word for it.

Thanks to my luck in passing the new 11-plus exam, I was one of the chosen few Gosport kids to be given a 'grammar school' education for free. We were the first full scholarship intake: until the advent of the 11-plus, parents had had to pay for a grammar-school place. For mine it might have seemed a blessing – but it wasn't an unalloyed joy.

"I'm so pleased with you," said Mum, unveiling the brand new, gleaming black Hercules bicycle, my reward for scoring high marks in an 'at-first-sight intelligence test' – similar to those our class had been practising every day for a year (still, only five out of 30 passed). My love of reading – the *Beano*, the *Dandy*, *Rupert*, schoolboy stories and adventure yarns – did it for me. I'd also got through a stack of obscure adult books, because until I went to the senior school I had no idea that Gosport had a children's library. None of the stern women who staffed the public library ever thought to mention it to me as I heaved some vast tome of Macaulay's *Essays* or Thomas De Quincey's *Memoirs of an English Opium Eater* onto the desk to get it stamped.

The downside of a scholarship to the grammar school, as my Dad – a man as near a Communist as a man could be without carrying a party card – was quick to note, was that we 'intelligent' ones would be taught to ape middle-class attitudes and values and therefore would grow away from our families. I can't recall all the many, many times over the next six years my mother Nell said to me: "I wish you'd never gone to that damned school."

Oh, I loved my family, still do. But I did suffer many young years of needlessly being ashamed of them – and even more ashamed of myself for it.

And that wasn't all. There may have been no fees to pay, but there was the uniform to buy, plus school satchels, sports gear, and so on, all available only from one Gosport shop, Hart's, who held a monopoly. And woe betide any kid whose desperate parent tried to provide a cheap alternative to, say, the regulation green blazer. The other kids made his life a misery until in desperation, the nipper managed to 'lose' the blazer, forcing his hard-up Mum into God knows what personal pain to raise the cash for a proper one. For some working mothers, I imagine it might have meant being obliged to stay on a bit late at work on a Friday to help the manager 'cash up' for an extra quid – if you get my drift.

Gosport County Grammar School's curriculum involved exotic subjects like French, Latin, Geometry, Algebra, Chemistry – and Physics, which in my ignorance I thought was a sort of Keep Fit. But the best bit for me was the school building itself – redbrick and white stucco in the Arts and Crafts style, with a circular tower at one end. It had been built in the early 1900s as a technical institute and still incorporated the Public Library. On the front elevation, facing the High Street, was a decorative bas relief depicting, in triumphal style, the landing of Bishop de Blois on the shores of Gosport. In grateful thanks to God for saving him from shipwreck, he named the place 'God's Port, Our Haven.'

A popular school joke had the Bishop, after his happy landing, taking one appalled look at the town and falling to his knees, saying: 'Lord, can we have another look at that chart?'

The ground floor housed two well-equipped laboratories, one for Chemistry and the other for Physics, and there was a Biology lab upstairs, alongside what was known as the Botany Corridor, a long working counter beneath a galleried window, with high-stools for students to sit on while dissecting little animals. The beautiful assembly hall rose two floors with a full-scale arched window at the west end. A balcony crossed the east end at first-floor level and under that balcony, every morning at break-time, the Tuck Shop would open, with one of the girl prefects selling buns and cakes at a penny a go. The classrooms were spacious and the art room ran the length of the frontage above the public library – with a copy of the mural reproduced in plaster on the inside.

The caretaker, the very model of his kind, lived in an apartment reached by the tower staircase, above the first floor. His name was Macduff, a tolerant man who smiled and nodded as each and every new teacher exercised their wit by misquoting Shakespeare: 'Lead on, Macduff.'

When I was in the third year, the school took over Bay House, the Sloane Stanley family's stately home which had been empty for some years and sold off to Hampshire County Council. It was beautifully located among the trees of Stanley Park at the western end of Stokes Bay. As far as we kids were concerned, it was paradise, a place to rival any public school for romantic surroundings – with none of the downside such as boarding and dormitories. It even had a moat at the end of the gardens on the south side.

We used to sit on the banks of the moat at lunchtimes, gazing out over the silvery Solent. A chance for the boys and girls to get together, though I was always a bit shy about these other creatures, especially the one I had fallen in love with and worshipped from afar – Brenda with the halo of dark curls and the very English complexion, a junior Jean Simmons. It was so lovely that in the summer term we often had lessons out on the lawns. Some of the rooms had been cleared of their original fittings to make way for classrooms. But there were still elegant bedrooms on the upper floors awaiting conversion. Like the school building in the High Street, Bay House also had a tower: I got in there once armed with a cavalry trumpet belonging to one of my classmates, climbed to the top, leaned out of the window and let rip my interpretation of the *The Charge* before the English master, Mr Hobbs, forced open the door and hustled me away.

The house was surrounded by beautiful parkland dotted with specimen trees. In the corner, with a terrace overlooking the bay, was the house built by the Stanleys for Edward VII to entertain his companion, Lily Langtry. Over the door was inscribed the Latin legend *Parva sed Apta* – Jersey Lily was quite tiny, too.

Bay House school

When I was 13, I was walking home from school one day with David Massey, who was two years older, and he asked me: "What are you going to do when you leave school?"

"Dunno. What are you going to do?"

"I'm going to be a journalist – you know, a newspaper reporter," he said.

"What exams do you have to take for that?"

"You don't take any – it's not like the Civil Service," he said.

A tiny seed lodged in my mind. I started to take more notice of the newspapers, notably the *Daily Herald* which Dad favoured, and on Sundays *The People*, along with the local papers – the *Portsmouth Evening News* and her sister paper, the *Hampshire Telegraph*, our local weekly which came out on Fridays. I saw a couple of newspaper films that came out around that time: these films always featured a brave, crusading journalist, usually played by, if not James Cagney, someone equally watchable. Finally I finished up reading autobiographies of journalists: *Ink in my Veins* by Cecil Hunt, and *I Found No Peace* by Webb Miller. There were novels too, the best of which was *The Street of Adventure* by Philip Gibbs.

In those days the careers advice in schools was non-existent. If our teachers ever thought about it at all it would have been more about how to get a job, not a career. Gosport kids who made it to grammar school were expected to be be pen-pusher fodder; in a navy town that generally meant a clerical job in the navy or in Her Majesty's Dockyard. Few school-leavers at 15 were thought of as officer material; and those that went on into the sixth form and took the Higher School Certificate were usually pointed towards an executive-level grade in the Civil Service. As for girls, they were expected to try nursing, teaching or secretarial, until marriage and child-rearing took care of the rest of their lives.

In the fifth form, just once, we were assembled in the hall at Bay House to hear a live(ish) civil servant address us on the subject of careers. It soon became pretty obvious that in his view O-levels meant a clerical job and A-levels meant a higher clerical job. My dear friend Ewart Colyer, who had political ambitions, eventually sank this time-serving wretch when he bluntly asked: "How do you go about becoming Prime Minister?" The entire room burst into unstoppable glee and that was the end of any state involvement in planning our future.

Almost every adult I asked about journalism said: "Well it's very hard to break into – you have to know someone on the inside." But when push came to shove, I found it simple enough. The best advisor I had, as on so many topics, was *Boy's Own Paper* which I had read every month since my Dad gave me a complete year's issues in 1944. Even if I couldn't afford to buy it, there was always a copy to be read at the library. For instance, when I was 15, I read a piece about panning for gold in mountain-streams – all you needed was a frying pan, half a potato and small phial of mercury. So in the Easter Hols I hitch-hiked to Wales, staying in Youth Hostels, and returned with a few golden flakes won from the river at Dolgelly, where the gold that was to be used for Her Majesty's wedding ring was mined.

The method was carefully explained in the magazine. You had to find an inside bend of the river with a sandbar. I spent hours peering into the sandy deposits, then used my small frying pan to pick up a sandy pint or so of water which I carefully swirled around, letting a little at a time pour back into the stream. Then, if the sun caught a glimpse of gold, a mere fleck maybe, I scooped it up and poured it into my spoil tin. This is easy to say, but it took long hours of painstaking work, my arms dropping off and my soul screaming with boredom before I had about an ounce of totally impure spoil, with tiny flecks that glinted in the sun (hopefully of gold and not iron pyrites, known as Fool's Gold).

After three or four days of this, I found a suitable spot along the riverbank, lit a fire and put the pan on to heat up. Meanwhile I added the tiny spoonfuls of impure dried spoil to a tiny bubble of mercury, mixing it thoroughly, and finally dropping it into the hot middle of the pan, then I clapped my hollowed-out half-potato over the blob, the mercury melted and became a gas that rose into the spud. This was then put aside to cool, eventually leaving a minute bubble of gold liquid, about the size of a pinhead. When it was quite cold, this was put in my 'winnings' tin, eventually to be given to Mum when I got home. Actual Welsh gold (or Welsh iron pyrites) – she kept it for years, referring to it as 'Nelly's Nugget'.

So when I read in my biblical *Boy's Own Paper* a letter from a lad who'd been taken on by his local paper to write-up football matches, I thought I'd have a go. Well before the summer holidays, I wrote to Mr Robinson, sports editor of the *Portsmouth Evening News* offering my services on Saturdays in the soccer season. He was quick to fix an appointment for me with Mr Collings, the senior reporter at the paper's district office in Gosport. Mr Collings was a ruddy-cheeked, well-spoken man, about 60, who chatted to me pleasantly. He outlined what the job entailed, then suggested they take me on trial starting in September when the local League games began again. He introduced me to his young deputy, Ted Brett, who would be my immediate boss.

I would be expected to turn out every Saturday to cover the Gosport League games at Gosport Park. There were never fewer than two games and sometimes three. I would take notes (Ted handed me a reporter's pocket-sized flip-over notebook), phone in a brief report at half-time and then phone in again with the full-time score for Saturday evening's sports paper, *Football Mail*. I had to submit a slightly longer report for Monday's *Evening News*, and a full 100-word report for the *Hampshire Telegraph*. I would be paid 7s 6d plus 1s for phone calls, in the form of a postal order for £1 11s every four weeks.

I couldn't believe it: I was on my way. I was one of those happy, happy people in the world who had found out what they wanted to do in life – and were young enough to go for it.

With this euphoric mood on me, I went straight over to the swimming pool, demanded to see the manager Ticker Weyman and asked for a job for the summer holidays. I got taken on at the princely sum of £2 10s a week.

Chapter Two
An Art Deco Summer

One day in my last summer at school sticks in my mind, not least because it was one of the very few, perfectly fine days we had in the whole damp, grey decade of the Fifties.

It was already hot as I cycled to Lee-on-the-Solent to my summer-holiday job at the swimming pool on the beach. In my youth, Lee always looked like the Thirties – a sort of pickled nostalgia that Gosport people thought would last for ever. I don't suppose Lee ever looked more *Art Deco* than on that bright, languorous August day. Sunshine gleamed on the landmark Tower, framed by an empty lavender sky, and the strong light glared back from the blanched seafront buildings with their concrete curves, flat roofs and metal-framed, porthole windows. For once, the sunshine hid the peeling paint, patches of rust, and all the stains and cracks of the neglected white façade. It was a Friday, payday: two pounds ten shillings.

The pool was to the west of the Tower at the foot of the earth cliffs, with concrete steps down to its gate. My boss, old Yorkie (who I always respectfully called Mr Stevens), was sweeping the steps down as I arrived.

The pool

"Tha' were reet to coom early, lad, be busy t'day," he said handing me the broom.

There wasn't much of him. An outdoor-man's leathery skin, tattoos faded to meaningless squiggles, his thick rubbery lips set in a walnut face. He was rumoured to be 90, admitted to 'gerrin' on a bit,' looked like a tortoise, and was as agile as a cat.

I went to help Dorrie, the lady who ran the snack bar. I took down the shutters, arranged a few tables and chairs, filled the big tea-urn and gladly accepted a cup of coffee. Yorkie spoiled it by reminding me that 't'brass' were coming today to inspect the place and telling me to trim the grass. This grass was the weed-covered, clay face of the cliff. It was almost vertical – hard enough to keep your footing on, without having to slash couch-grass with a sickle. Yorkie did it by moving crabwise with knees bent, steadily cutting in a smooth arc.

"Get theesen into a swing, lad," he had said on my first day. Over the weeks, we had so much rain that I got plenty of practice. I didn't do it well, but I did do it quickly.

By eleven it was sweltering, as Yorkie unlocked the gate and I took up my place in the hut with a roll of tickets and a stout leather shoulder bag for the money – 3d entrance, 6d for a deckchair. Toddlers went to the paddling pool at the far end, older kids into the big one that sloped from 3ft to 5ft, and was about 50ft long. For once we were all busy. Yorkie supervised the pools; Dorrie sold ice-cream, tea, coffee and cakes. Over the damp summer weeks, when trade was either slack or non-existent, they habitually vanished, leaving me alone in my box. I read a lot, occasionally had a swim, and learned to tell the time without a watch by clocking the Hants and Dorset buses to Hill Head, Stubbington, Titchfield and Fareham, one of which passed along the road above us every quarter of an hour.

At noon Ticker Weyman, the council baths superintendent from Gosport, came with our wages and took samples from the pool to test the water quality. I had just let in a bunch of kids from the children's orphanage holiday home on the seafront – forgetting to charge them, of course – and was munching one of Dorrie's sandwiches when Yorkie brought me the bad news.

"Ticker wants uz to clean t'pool s'afternoon," he said.

This I'd been warned about. Since the pool was fed by the sea, the bottom attracted an intensive growth of weed and, despite filters, a fair bit of muck. Cleaning meant letting all the water out on the ebb tide, then scrubbing the bottom, ready to refill.

"I'll start draining about 'alf past three," Yorkie said. "So the kids can have their foon while teatime. It taks an hour or more to empty. Then thee and me'll start scroobin."

This was not a happy prospect. Not much good having two pound ten burning a hole in my pocket if I was going to be stuck here half the evening.

As the afternoon grows hotter, demand at the café warms up. Yorkie takes over the hut, while I am sent to the Tower to get more ice-cream for Dorrie. Half the population of Gosport seems to be on the shingle beach, especially the bit around the barnacled ruin of the pier. There's a distinct generation-clash between young girls in itsy-bitsy, polka-dot bikinis who are lying in the sun, and older parties with skirts or trousers rolled up to paddle in the sea. The Tower is doing a roaring trade with people buying threepenny tickets for the lift to the top to admire the view over the sparkling Solent.

The manager Mr Fleming takes me to a storeroom and gives me a large biscuit tin full of ice-creams from the fridge. The frost bites straight through my thin shirt as I hug it to my chest. In my hurry, I march straight across the ballroom.

"What the hell do you think you're doing?" roars Fleming. To my dismay, my beach shoes are leaving a wide trail of damp sand across the floor of his newly polished dance floor. Flight is the only answer and I charge out the door and along the clifftop.

Back at the pool, I'm shivering with the cold and Dorrie has to peel the tin away from my chest. She offers me an ice-cream which I decline in favour of a hot cup of tea. The customers are drifting away as the falling water-level reveals the slimy state of the pool. As the last water drains out, Yorkie fits up a hose ready for us to scrub the weed and muck off the bottom. He changes into leather boots with nailed soles. I put on my swimming trunks.

"That bottom's a sheet o'glass as you'll soon find out," Yorkie says. "Yer'll need to stick a couple of stones under yer toes to get a grip, lad." He goes out over the shingle and hunts down a couple the right size and shape.

"Coom 'ere, lad. Get 'old of t'broom, keep it straight in front o'thee. Mek a long stroke, bring broom back and bang it down to shake off t'muck, then another long stroke. Lean on t'broom, keep yer feet on t'deck, and keep pushing t'muck forward towards the drain in't middle."

He demonstrates, working from the sides inwards towards the drain. I put the stones under my toes, grip them hard and slide the broom forward. My feet slide and I'm sitting in a pool of water with a wet bum. Then, without warning, Yorkie gives a yelp as his feet shoot from under him. He lands on his shoulders and the back of his head hits the concrete with a crack I swear I can hear. He doesn't get up, and the water flowing from the hose quickly turns red. I leap out of the pool and run for the first-aid box. Quick-witted Dorrie takes one look and phones for a taxi.

Yorkie sits up, staring at his blood pouring all over the pool. Dorrie slaps a thick dressing over his wound and sticks it to his bald pate with plasters. And somehow we get him to the gate and into a cab, to take him to a doctor to stitch him up.

I went back to the scrubbing. After half-an-hour my toes stopped hurting and simply went numb. I slipped a few times, indeed I fell a lot at the start. Gradually, slowly, I managed to keep going: push-slide forward, grip tight, bang down broom, push-slide again, working clockwise round the pool. The sun stopped warming my bare shoulders.

It was late when I finally prized the stones from under my cramped, tortured toes, washed the last bits of muck down the drain, and put all the gear away. I was covered in filth and ached everywhere. I limped down the shingle beach to meet the now-incoming tide and threw myself into the waves. The sea was warm: I kicked out, rolled on my back and looked up at the stars coming out. The aches and pains just floated away.

For the first time in my life I felt that delicious, satisfying tiredness that only comes after a really hard day's work.

Ian Plowman's portrait of Michael Gabbert in hard-bitten reporter mode

Chapter Three
Saturday at the Park

That September I began my newspaper career covering every Saturday football game at Gosport Park, never less than two and sometimes three in an afternoon. I biked over to the park on that first Saturday with a nor'easter taking the edge off the autumn sunshine, blowing straight across Haslar creek. In my pocket was my brand new flipover Reporter's Notebook, provided by Ted Brett.

As I arrived, I noticed a muscular lad with a mane of blond hair cruising through the park on a girl's bike, and recognised him as Michael Gabbert, the junior reporter who I'd glimpsed a couple of times going into or coming out of the *News* office in Gosport – obviously he'd been sent to make sure I was in place.

He rode off without even a wave. Neither of us knew it but – as Bogart says to Claude Rains in the classic film *Casablanca* – 'I think this is the beginning of a beautiful friendship.' We were to be close at work or play, for nearly 40 years, until his untimely death in 1988. Events with Michael were sometimes emotional, sometimes sensational, sometimes dangerous, sometimes just hilarious – but never, ever dull.

Back to the touchline. The teams in the Gosport League that I covered were named for local firms and Admiralty bases, like Camper and Nicholson, Arrow Athletic, AWRE and Fleetlands. There was also Clarence A – a school old boys' team – and Stubbington Covenanters, a brave free church outfit that I once saw beaten 22-0. Hammered but not humiliated, they later, after a full season without a win, were given a prize for sporting attitude from the *News Chronicle*, a Fleet Street paper of the day.

These Gosport teams usually had a team manager or club secretary on the touchline to cheer players on, and maybe a girlfriend and some mates, brave souls. It was obvious I needed help, so I cultivated these supporters – on both sides, of course – moving from one to the other as goals or near misses occurred. That way, I got the name of the scorer or goalie.

It was OK when there was plenty of action: 'Arrow showed spirit in attack, Campers were pinned back – a neat pass from Hatton gave Ron Breeze his chance and the league's top scorer added another to his tally'. Goals were more frequent than they are today, but penalties were as rare as five pound notes. I don't recall anyone being sent off.

I soon found I only needed one incident to cover my half-time phone piece for the evening's *Football Mail*....then to add the final scoreline at the end. But I also had to find enough to cover my 100 words for Friday's *Hampshire Telegraph* and, of course I had to keep my ears and eyes open for interesting bits and pieces of news for 'Ted's Shots at Goal' round-up in the following week's *Football Mail*. This could include snippets about the players, such as who was getting married or becoming a dad, preferably, as Ted said, in that order.

I thought I'd be bored after a few games, but I have to say I thoroughly enjoyed describing football – along with the anticipation of the evening to come with my girlfriend Nancy. There's a lot to be said for the knowledge you are going to spend the evening cuddling your sweetheart when you standing on a football pitch with a shrill nor'easter blowing straight through you.

Of course I was still at school, so during the week there was Bay House – not yet properly coverted into classrooms. We revelled in the posh, aristocratic setting, the Dutch gardens and spacious lawns among great oak trees, all set off by the background of the wide and restless sea. Imagine relaxing in an easy chair in front of a comforting coal fire with something you'll only find in the best stately homes – a big window above the fireplace, fascinatingly set in the middle of the chimney. How did they do that?

I treasure the memory of that blissful last autumn at school, as a sixth-former and a prefect. It was a delicious time-out-of-time as we studied different aspects of European history and literature in both English and French. From the rumbustious, romantic, often crude but very human poets like François Villon or Geoffrey Chaucer, to that master-of-masters for elegance and knockabout comedy combined, William Shakespeare.

The company was pretty good, too. The teachers were interesting people in their own right: Teddy Tanton (History), a dominant figure in the school hierarchy and a born organiser; John Caroll and Barbara Thompson (French); 'Milly' Millington and the glamorous Joan Howell (English). They treated me and my mates as equals as we argued over *The Winter's Tale* or *Antony and Cleopatra*. Then there was the sheer joy of Thomas Hardy: I'd read every word he left for us by the time I quit school. My love of Dickens was born then too, though it didn't mature until years later.

My nostalgia for that autumn may also be governed for me by the green shoots of first love. Somehow I had been cured of my fear of girls by the delicate charm of Nancy, who I first dared to chat to while waiting for a bus outside Bay House. She had the face and figure of a Hollywood actress I favoured, Wanda Hendrix (who often played the teenage romantic lead in Westerns), coupled with, as I discovered as we abandoned the bus and walked across the fields, a down-to-earth attitude and a spiky sense of humour.

Furthermore I was surprised to find she didn't actually think I was repulsive or boring. She had left school in the summer and become a student at Portsmouth's College of Art. So the autumn term found me getting the bus to Fareham, five miles away, to visit her at the bungalow where she lived with her mother. We used to sit at either end of the long sitting-room sofa, listening to AFN, the American Forces Network aimed at GIs stationed in Europe, getting the latest US hits and some magic jazz.

I had to share Nancy with a couple of rivals from her old class at school. One of these was a cheery lad much given to scientific experiment. He had recently blown part of his face off making fireworks. Worryingly, Nancy told me later that he'd landed a job at Aldermaston, Britain's hush-hush atomic weapons establishment. It probably turned out all right though. If not, I think we might have heard....

My wonderful autumn was also enlivened by a week off school undergoing aptitude tests for a short service commission in the RAF. At that time all of us lads were called up to do two years' National Service for a lousy £1 10s a week, a full pound less than I'd been getting for sweeping up at the swimming pool. However, with a commission you got a more reasonable wage. Gosport being a serviceman's town, a fair number of my contemporaries took up the offer, either in the RAF or the Royal Navy's Fleet Air Arm.*

I arrived at Hornchurch, in Essex, on a Monday morning, carrying an over-sized suitcase – more of a cabin trunk really – which my father had bought in Shanghai in the 1930s. A handful of other blokes of the school prefect caste were already standing outside the railway station grouped around a couple of RAF NCOs, waiting to be loaded on a bus and taken to the RAF base. This gave the sergeant in charge a cheap laugh as he pointed to my trunk and said: 'See you're used to roughing it then, milord'.

All 12 of us were billeted in a typical service hut with iron-framed beds and rock-hard mattresses. But they worked us hard enough to make us sleep well.

---

* Eight to ten fellows from my school volunteered to fly either with the RAF or the Fleet Air Arm. Of these at least four died in flying accidents. Another chap landed his jet on top of two others on the ground, wrecking all three. He, however, walked away.

There were the usual intelligence tests, which probably gave scholarship boys like me, accustomed to this type of test, a somewhat unfair advantage over the precious ones whose parents had paid for their public school places. One aptitude test sticks in my mind. We had to sit down in front of a pegboard containing 50 pegs. Each peg was topped with a circular head, half-black, half white. As a test of dexterity we had to take them out, turn them round and replace them, trying to do as many as possible in one minute. Simple. I think we managed to average about 30. And then they told us that the record stood at 126 turnrounds. That victorious candidate had finally admitted he was a packer in a biscuit factory on piecework.

The medicals were the most exacting part – these doctors checked everything. And, of course, after a long cross-country run, they tested us all again.

We were divided into teams, given a rope and an empty barrel, and told to get our team across a stream at the back of the airfield – said to contain radioactive material, piranha fish and man-eating sharks. The examiners wandered around with clipboards watching all the time, presumably to see if any of us could keep a straight face.

As usual in this sort of group one bloke seemed determined to be head boy – possibly he had the job at his (as he soon told us) public school. He managed to recruit a couple of the others, who soon showed they were ready to suck-up to him. By the second evening of our stay he had gathered about half of the set around him and was pontificating on all sorts of subjects as we supped our halves of shandy or cider in the Naafi Club (a feature of every RAF base). The rest of us remained steadfastly independent, and I figured they felt as wary as me of trying too hard to be popular. In my case, I was too uncertain of myself to do anything else.

I had a bit of a shock when just before our results were announced I got a call to see the president of the medical assessment board. He turned out to be a shrewd Irishman.

"Did you make a mistake on the form where you put down a mastoid operation for 1939 – did you mean 1949?"

"No sir, I was four at the time."

"You realise that such an op might rule out flying duties?"

"Well, sir, as far as I know the operation was a complete success. The surgeon apparently was proud of his work, or so they said," I told him, inwardly marvelling at having the guts to say it.

The doc smiled.

"OK – we'll assume that since you've had no trouble for more than ten years, you're fine. But don't blame me if your eardrums burst when you go into a dive." I caught the twinkle in his eye and promised not to complain.

"By the way, who prescribed reading glasses for you?"

"Our optician," I said, "he's my uncle – he thought I needed them because I read a great deal."

"Your uncle, eh? Ignore him. Throw the glasses away. I'm quite sure you don't need them. Your eyesight is pretty well as perfect as it gets – and eyes are my specialty."

He gave me a chit that said my physical condition was A1 G1.

"We find 90 percent of the boys who come here fail the medical, by the way," he added.

The euphoria didn't hit me until next morning over breakfast in the mess. Late September sunshine was glittering all over the airfield and its vista of trees and distant, gentle hills. I felt an easy sense of relaxed wellbeing. I wasn't just happy: suddenly I felt I had a right to be happy. It was a moment to cling to. Imagine – you are about to take on the world and you've just been told you are in perfect health. At that moment I didn't give a damn about the rest of the tests. I was already flying....

We were a good entry: six of our 12 were selected and we held a quiet celebration in the Naafi on our last evening. The public school boy failed the medical – he and the other five left Hornchurch earlier in the afternoon. I left in the morning armed with an official invitation to apply for aircrew training when I reached the age of 18 next summer.

My ex-matelot dad had mixed feelings. He was proud of me, of course, but he didn't much fancy having a 'Rupert' for a son.

Chapter Four
A Real Job

Ted Brett lived only a few streets away, so I used to drop off my copy for the *Hampshire Telegraph*, plus any 'Shots at Goal' I'd found, at his home on Sunday around teatime.

"Come on in," he said, on a chilly December day. His wife Audrey (whose sister Joan turned out to work in Clarence Yard with my father) asked: "Would you like a cuppa? We're just going to have one." Turned out there was a thick slice of her wonderful fruit cake on offer, too.

Ted looked up from leafing through my reports. "Yes, this is good stuff, y'know. Ever wanted to work on a paper?"

"Well, yes, I like the idea. In fact that's why I was so pleased to get the Saturday job."

"Thought so," Ted said with his trademark grin. "I think you'd be right for it. There is a vacancy coming for a new junior and if you like I'm happy to recommend you to Taffy Symons, the editor."

I was knocked sideways. "Hey that would be great, Ted. I'd love to have a shot at it – if you think I'd be any good."

"Whoa back, it's not a done deal you understand – but I think I can get Mr Collings to back you as well. He's the chief reporter for Gosport. They'll at least have you in for an interview."

Newspaper men tend not to hang about, and next Friday saw me at the head office of the *Evening News* in Stanhope Road – right opposite Portsmouth's main railway station. There was a tall lad hanging about in the corridor outside the editor's office on the first floor.

"Hello," he said. "You for interview? They said there was another victim coming in. I'm Roy West."

I introduced myself and wished him luck, with the mental proviso – 'just so long as you come second.'

"There's only one vacancy I'm told," I said.

"Yeah – you done much photography?"

"Er, no. Do we have to take photos as well?"

He looked puzzled. "Hang on – I'm here for the junior photographer's job. Aren't you?"

"I'm here for the reporter's job," I said, "They didn't tell me about the photographer's one."

Mr Symons, whom I was later to call Taffy as everyone else did (though not to his face of course), treated me very courteously, and asked the routine set of interview questions. Then without comment he sent me to see Mr Williams, the deputy general manager.

After a short wait he called me in.

"Mr Symons is happy to offer you an apprenticeship as a junior reporter."

I stammered out some sort of thanks and then went into a daze while he explained the apprenticeship terms and drafted a formal letter for my father to sign.

Finally he said: "You will be expected to wear a suit and preferably a clean white shirt...." then he smiled, shook my hand and surprised me by adding: "I believe you are related to Jim Wolland, the sportsman?"

I must have mentioned this to Ted.

"He's my Uncle Jim," I said simply.

"Great friend of mine in our younger days," said Mr Williams. "Give him my regards when you see him."

Since Uncle Jim was very active in local sport, it wasn't long before I did.

Later, of course, I often worked with Roy West or met him at parties and we often regaled colleagues with the story of how we joined the *News* on the same day. We always said we had tossed a coin to see who went for which vacancy – with the knockout punchline:

"Pity we got that the wrong way round then!"

My long-suffering parents were pleased that I'd got my dream job. They never said so, but they must have been greatly relieved I was going to earn money and that there was hope of the cuckoo leaving the nest one day.

I started on £2 5s a week (five bob less than I got at the swimming pool) with a rise to about £4 after three months, when I would also qualify to share in the quarterly bonus, which depended on the newspaper's financial results but was usually equivalent to a week's pay. It was agreed that I pay my mother £1 10s a week board and lodging – a bargain. In fact, when I finally married she presented me with a set of National Savings Certificates for a very handsome sum – the money I'd paid her over the years, plus interest.

By now the school Christmas holidays had begun, so I had to go to the home of our headmaster Mr Alan Walker in Beech Grove, Alverstoke, regarded as the poshest part of town, to break the news that I was leaving to become a cub reporter. He took it on the chin with his usual *sang froid*.

"I wish you luck, Baker," he said without a blink. He'd often confused me with my classmate Alan Baker – and I have to say that in our school photograph I have trouble myself deciding who is which. Though Hooky Walker did get my name right the last time we met, in 1961. We bumped into each other on a train and he asked what I was doing these days.

"I'm off to Paris to work for the French News Agency," I said.

"Good Lord – where did you learn the language?"

I've never been sure whether he was joking or not.

One thing I am sure of – Ted Brett did me the favour of a lifetime.

The imposing Victorian frontage. Photograph courtesy of *The News*, Portsmouth

Chapter Five
A Murder in Week Three

I was due to start work at 9am on Thursday January 1, 1953 (New Year's Day was not designated a Bank Holiday in England until 1974). I arrived at Gosport ferry pontoon in good time and asked for a ticket to Portsmouth.

This was the first shock. All my life the passenger fare to Pompey had been one penny. Suddenly it had gone up, by a shocking 50 percent, to a penny ha'penny. This was a short, sharp signal that my dreamy childhood was over and I was staring stark reality in the face.

Arriving at Stanhope Road, I stopped to admire the imposing Victorian facade with the name of the paper in big gold letters across the front. On the ground floor was the commercial office, the splendour of its business-like black railings and grilles reminding me of an old-fashioned bank. In contrast, the reporters' room upstairs was straight out of a 1930s Hollywood newspaper film and was overpoweringly black and white. Individual desks were ranged in two columns down the sides with the chief reporter's long desk at the top end under a dramatic panoramic window. This overlooked the Guildhall Square – centre of the city's beating heart – the Town railway station, the criss-cross of tramways to all parts, and a dominating statue of Queen Victoria....not counting the wreck of the once beautiful Guildhall destroyed by German bombs in the Blitz and not yet repaired.

Each reporter's desk had a heavy upright typewriter, Olympia or Remington, an oversized black GPO telephone and an iron-framed swivel chair. The room was full of reporters typing or talking on the phone.

I was shown the sub-editors' room – a hushed, cathedral-like space with men bent over bits of paper – the photo department, and the Creed room, where batteries of teleprinter machines brought news from all over Britain, and indeed the world, courtesy of the Press Association, the Exchange Telegraph Company and Reuter's. There was also a section with girls at typewriters, all wearing headsets and taking down copy phoned in by journalists out on the job or in district offices.

Over everything hung the heady, never-to-be-forgotten odour of printer's ink – for me and many like me the most fragrant, powerful scent ever. I have only to close my eyes and conjure a picture of any of the nine or ten newsrooms I've haunted in my time, for the whiff of printer's ink to rise in my nostrils. I really believe I can smell it.

Hot metal: plate-makers at work in the foundry. Photograph courtesy of *The News*, Portsmouth

Overawed by this Caliph's palace, I walked down the long reporters' room, on chessboard black-and-white squared lino, to the desk of Mr Bloomfield – Old Bloomy – the chief reporter, a bluff, heavily-built man in his fifties. He showed me The Diary, more important to reporters than the Holy Bible. There was a long list of tasks for the day, Thursday, alongside which were the initials of the reporter covering the event. Near the top of the list, just under the line that said Police Calls, was printed Hospital Calls and against that – Miss Phillips and JB. Bloomy looked over to a tall, dark-haired, willowy girl (the only girl in the room) and said "Miss Phillips, this is Mr John Bull. Please take him to the hospitals and show him what to do."

Off we went down the narrow staircase to the side alley – the reporters' special entrance. Later I was to be entrusted with my own key for use out of business hours, in the evenings or Sundays. On the way to the Royal Hospital in Mile End, Pat told me her father was a journalist, the well-known *Daily Mirror* sports writer Tom Phillips. She hoped to join him at the best-selling daily when she got her 'Big Break'.

I soon discovered over coffee, or a pint in the Bass House, one of the three or four pubs within hailing distance of the office, that all reporters shared the same dream – always looking for that Big Break, the Great Scoop, the exclusive splash story that would make our name. I also learned that we never wrote 'reports' – everything, big or small, was 'a story'.

In that first week I prepared the Ships That Pass column from a list of navy and mercantile vessels entering or leaving harbour – that, and writing up an endless round of children's Christmas parties given by big firms, shops like the Landport Drapery Bazaar or the many navy and Royal Marine establishments around the city (Christmas parties went on until February in Pompey in those times).

"Three pars maximum," Bloomy warned me. "Last par the names of everyone, repeat everyone, who had a hand in organising the event. Leave out a name, they'll hate the paper and never, ever buy it again." I got the message.

On Miss Phillips' day off I got to do the hospital calls and the follow-ups to the homes of people who had been involved in accidents or emergencies, such as a kid getting his head jammed in a saucepan. Bigtime for the new cub reporter.

I tell a lie. There was one big chance for me after a mere three weeks. If I were to mention, casually in conversation, that in my third week as a reporter (aged 17) I covered a murder, I can count on two distinct reactions:

'What a liar this bloke is'....or....a nod and a sympathetic smile – that, of course, will be from any fellow journalist.

Newspapers were firmly embedded in the 'sit down next to Nellie and do what she does' school of training, which always included a sadistic streak of 'throw 'em in – see if they float'. It was Monday morning: I had just finished typing out the Ships That Pass column for the next day's *News* and was taking it to the chief reporter, who was talking on the phone. Abruptly he hung up and called over Peter Jones, a senior reporter.

"Miss Phillips on police calls says they had a 999 call round midnight – three kids found dead, possibly murdered, and their mother taken to hospital in a coma. Here's my notes," he said handing over a scribbled list. "Take Mr Gabbert with you to help with any legwork. And phone as soon as you get there. Oh....and take Mr Bull with you – it'll be useful training for him."

That last bit being newsroom code for 'keep him out of my hair for a while'.

The paper's chief photographer, Vic Stewart, came into the reporters' room and offered to drive us up to the scene, a set of married quarters, lined up with military precision in a street in Hilsea. A solitary PC stood guard outside one of them. Vic immediately snapped off a picture of the scene of the crime.

Jones said: "We'll divide up these houses and start knocking on doors. If you two get anything, come and tell me."

Gabbert and I started with the homes on either side. Jones nodded to the copper on guard and went to chat to him. A nervy-sounding woman answered my knock by shouting through the letterbox:

"I'm only looking after the house. The couple from here are down at number 2 having a cup of tea."

There was no sign of Jones or Gabbert, or Vic, so I moved down to number 2 and tapped gently on the front-room window. The front door opened and an anxious chap with the look of a serviceman peered out.

"I'm from the *News*," I said. "Can I come in and have a chat?"

Two women came in from the kitchen and offered me a cup of tea and I sat down with them. One of them told me tearfully that she was the next-door neighbour of the family.

"What happened to the children?" I asked. And then it all came tumbling out – they'd been found gassed.

"It was just before midnight," she said. "We heard this gasping noise from next door – it was a kind of murmur. It was my husband who called the police. They found two of the boys, aged 11 and 10, dead on the bedroom floor, and the youngest, aged two, dead in bed, and the mother in a coma."

At this point she broke down. The neighbours moved to comfort her. And I found myself in the kitchen making more tea.

They told me the family had come to live there two years ago, and seemed very happy. The mother, 'a coloured woman from Nairobi' they said, often complained that people were watching her and following her around, though lately she had been pleased that her husband, serving in Germany, was returning home soon. They believed his service time was nearly up.

Jones and Gabbert were waiting for me down the road and Jones was delighted with the story I'd got from the neighbour. He copied down my 'interview' and went off to the phone-box to call it in.

Gabbert and I made our way back to the office. When the city edition was handed out as usual in the Reporters' Room, I found the story was the splash:

Three Hilsea Boys Found Dead
Policewoman at mother's bedside *

As Gabbert said, as we strolled round to Verrecchia's for tea: "Yet another tragic story of poor buggers unable to cope with reality...."

Abruptly, he stopped at the phone-box just outside the café.

"Here! We haven't showed you how to make free phone calls, have we?"

He crowded me into the phone-box and lifted the receiver. Then he tapped the receiver rest, while counting aloud: "Two, two, one, one."

He held up the receiver so I could hear: there was a brief ringing tone and a girl's voice said: "Hello. Evening News."

Gabbert said: "Hello Peggy, Mike here. Can you put me through to Gosport 8930, please?"

After a slight pause, I heard someone answer, "Hello, Gosport Town Hall." Gabbert then replaced the receiver.

"Simple," he said. "An engineer showed me. You just tap in the number on the receiver rest – the only tricky bit is that you have to do it at the rate of ten beats per second. Makes the *News* number 2211 easy, but it can be tricky knocking out anything above eight.

"Needs a bit of practice. But you can see how we do it – tap in 2211 to get our switchboard and then ask the girl for the number you want. Try it."

I did. And it worked. I used the system the whole time I was on the paper and it saved a small fortune in fourpences – at the time, the price of a call.

The office was a source of great satisfaction to me. I loved its film-set quality. I admired the fact that hot water came out of the taps in the washroom – not something I had been used to at home. I loved the background sound of the presses drumming away two floors down in the basement, and the teleprinters chuntering in the Creed room.

---

* An inquest found the boys died from gas poisoning. At the County Assizes, their mother was declared unfit to face charges.

Just like the movies: the sub-editors at work

I found excuses to go into the sub-editors' room, where the older members of the editorial staff waded through acres of reporters' copy (to our minds, slashing and burning anything that smacked of excitement and turning it all into a sort of bureaucratic dross. If you'd heard us talking about it in the pub, that would be the impression you'd come away with).

I did occasionally meet these chaps as well as the 'commercials' and the inkies from below in the hallowed machine room, face to face in the remarkable office canteen, which was on an upper floor with a view to the west over Pompey's lovely Victoria Park. Here presided the case-hardened Mrs T. I never discovered her full name. For a shilling or so you could eat meat, spuds and two veg, followed by apple tart and custard, all washed down by half a pint of tea. Wonderful. But the best bit was always the gossip. Rumours and slurs got a regular airing – all part of the service.

In my first week Old Bloomy called me over to 'discuss' my time off.

"Now Mr Bull," he said, "I'm going to give you Thursday afternoons off, as you are entitled to each week. If you work Sundays, or have more than two night jobs in any week, you will be entitled to a full day off. However, since we are short-handed these days it would be wiser not to rely on that, eh?"

"Oh no, Mr Bloomfield," I told him brightly, "I quite understand. Only too happy to carry on."

Neither of us was terribly convinced, but that's the way it was.

And so that is how I became a great fan of the glorious French cinema of the Fifties – *La Nouvelle Vague* as it came to be reverently admired. On Thursdays after my canteen lunch, rather than nip back to Gosport, I used to while away the afternoon at the pictures, usually the Palace in Commercial Road, where foreign movies were shown. The Palace, which had a swastika-style cross set in the floor-tiles at the entrance, was noted for its 'dirty mac' clientele.

There I saw the great French classics – *Le salaire de la peur (The Wages of Fear)* with Yves Montand, *Rififi, The Sheep Has Five Legs* with Fernandel – as well as a stack of comedies featuring the redoubtable Louis de Funês, and of course my all-time favourite *Rue de L'Estrapade (Françoise Steps Out)* with Anne Vernon *and* Georges Brassens singing his masterpiece *Le Parapluie* (played in the movie by Daniel Gélin). Thanks, Bloomy.

Perhaps the best thing was that my girlfriend Nancy, now a student at Portsmouth College of Art, was impressed with my new status.

"Do they just accept you – as a reporter, I mean?" she asked.

"Well, I go to the police station or the hospitals and ask if anything has happened. Write it down and go back to the office, write it up as a story and then it appears in print."

"What – they print the report just as you wrote it?"

"Well more or less. They seem to have their own newspaper language. They don't call it a report by the way – everything we write is a 'story.' We don't always have time to go back to the office to write, say if we are going on to the magistrates court, so we might stop off for a quick coffee in Verrecchia's...."

"That's where all us art students go."

"I know. Probably see you in there, then. More likely in the afternoon for tea – you lazy lot aren't likely to be there at nine thirty in the morning, are you?"

We did indeed often meet at Verrecchia's wonderful ice-cream parlour, under the trees on the edge of the city's wide Guildhall Square. It had mahogany booths, marble-topped tables and decorative *art nouveau* glass dividers, steaming coffee machines and wonderful ice-cream concoctions. For years it was the resort for 'artists' or musicians and other idlers with too much to say, including the more exotic students from the art college and the Municipal College, or 'Muni'.

Naturally the reporters found it a great source of 'contacts'. Reputations were made and lost over drinks on the marble table-tops, always under the watchful eye of 'Tony' (real name Gus) the dapper moustachioed boss, or his three slender, dark-haired, dark-eyed, pouting daughters. Of course we lads tried, but could never really get near them – it would have been like trying to date the Mafia.

One jarring note to my new life was the unexpected news that we young reporters – the apprentices – were expected to attend an out-station of the Muni to improve our education every Friday afternoon. This was a new initiative of the National Union of Journalists and the Newspaper Society, the bosses' union, called the National Council for the Training of Journalists (NCTJ).

This half-day release was aimed at taking exams in three years' time for a Proficiency Certificate. We lads – and by now we had two female juniors, Pat Phillips having been joined by Ena Naunton, a secretary on the commercial side who fancied a change of pace – thought this was a total waste of time and, being resourceful people, we managed to skip quite a few sessions, taking it in turns to bunk off.

Two typical male teachers, tweedy heroes with a pipe stuck in their jacket pocket, took us through the curriculum – Mr Jenkins, an amiable Welshman doing English and Economics, and the forgettable, serious one so boring I've forgotten his name, teaching Law for Journalists, and the British Constitution, which we renamed (cue African native accent) 'De Queen done reign – but she am not de gubbernor.'

I'd already done the first year of A-level English and History so I found those bits easy and eventually passed those exams without raising a sweat. I also discovered an interest in Economics and passed that one with distinction (having, I admit, borrowed the notes of a mate who was doing Economics at university, and read them thoroughly the day and most of the night before the exam). Go on, ask me about the law of diminishing returns – it's still my best party piece.

We all eventually got our Proficiency Certificate, though one guy who missed the English exam altogether was awarded a pass, and another who had done the exam was failed. Typical, I discovered, of the British exam system.

It's fair to say that no editor has ever asked me if I have this proficiency certificate. They used to prefer to talk to you and make up their own minds whether or not you were a reporter – as indeed, so did I when my turn came.

Chapter Six
Can't Touch Me, I'm Part of the Union

My period of probation ran out after three months and I was invited to join the pension scheme – and also the National Union of Journalists. Actually neither of these was truly voluntary. It was made clear to me that this was a union house – 'a closed shop' – so, of course, I joined and started paying in my modest subs out of my new-found wealth, my pay having been raised to £4 a week. Better still, I was now eligible to be part of the profit-sharing scheme which paid out a quarterly bonus.

Union meetings were held monthly in one of the pubs in nearby Edinburgh Road, opposite the Coliseum Theatre, where there are still four pubs in a row: the Royal Standard, the Park Tavern, the Trafalgar and the Shipwright's Arms. Most of us juniors attended – chiefly for the chat and to hear the stories of the old hands. First there was the *Evening News* Chapel meeting, led by the Father and the Clerk, our elected officials (throughout my apprenticeship, the same two blokes held the posts). That usually took no more than half an hour, as we discussed items like asking management to replace the spent light-bulb at the top of the reporters' side entrance (strangely enough this item was nearly always on the agenda at every local newspaper I ever worked for – plus a couple of big-time Fleet Street titles. Mean bastards).

Chapel meetings only concerned conditions and events at the News, Chapel relations with NUJ nationally, and relations with local government. I remember some acid battles with Hampshire County Council, especially the Education Committee (notable for its collection of belted earls and other landed gentry), who seemed to think that what went on in county schools was no business of the Press, and certainly not the public. What was the country coming to? They had a habit of not replying to our letters.

The Portsmouth NUJ branch meeting, which dealt with wider issues, then followed, led by the chairman Dennis Tressider, the national paper freelance, and the treasurer and secretary Jerry Diddymus, known as Young Diddy, because he was the son of Old Diddy, national treasurer of the NUJ itself. Both of them were freelances too, but specialising in the trade press – in those days far more extensive and therefore more lucrative for freelances than today.

We junior reporters (the term 'cub reporter' had dropped out of use while I was a probationer) looked forward to these meetings, especially the sessions in the pub afterwards where we'd pick up the finer points of the game from the old-timers, especially in regard to expenses claims, time-off entitlements and lineage compensation.

Lineage – selling stories to publications other than your employer – was regarded by journalists as a Bad Thing/Good Thing depending on your likelihood of being in a position to have something to sell. You might stumble on a court case shocking enough to make the *Daily Mirror*, or dirty enough for the *News of the World* where the sky was the limit, or it could be an ordinary little case involving a man from, say, Southampton, which you could then send to the *Southern Daily Echo* and be paid a guinea or so. All these payments were calculated in guineas (£1.1s), right up until decimalisation.

The position in Portsmouth had recently been changed. Management had got the *News* Chapel to agree to a deal whereby, in exchange for a regular additional payment, their members agreed not to touch lineage. Junior reporters received an increment of five shillings; senior reporters and sub-editors up to three guineas a week.

We juniors argued that since we were the foot-soldiers on the front line we were in a better place to sell our stories (it was the custom in the trade that you didn't do that until it had appeared in your own paper) and therefore were entitled to more compensation. The chairbound sub-editors countered with the fact that under the old lineage system, they each held a 'contract' with certain papers. Whoever phoned in the story, had do it in the name of a particular sub. The sub would then pass on a part of the payment – usually less than half – to the reporter. This system was known as 'milking' a reporter's work. Suffice to say that this controversy lasted all my time at the *News*. Portsmouth was known as a goldmine for any freelance in the city – there was no competition and later on, the lone correspondent (or 'cor') for Fleet Street papers grew into a full agency of two or three, plus a freelance photographer.

By the time I was working out of the Gosport office, I was picking up half-a-guinea a week for not doing lineage, which greatly amused my Dad: he thought it wonderful that here was a lad being paid extra for doing nothing. I believe that the *News* was the only paper in Britain operating this system at the time.

One day when I was sent to cover Gosport Magistrates Court I was joined at the Press table by an unshaven, middle-aged cove in a grubby mac.

"You from the *News*?" he asked. I nodded.

"I'm Jim Rudd – freelance, just moved into the area," he said, shoving a hand my way.

I took it half-heartedly, noticing the bitten-down nails, the inkspots, and the frayed cuff of the shirt. At the end of the court session, as we left the building, he announced that he was living in Titchfield and covering 'South Hampshire' for the nationals. If I liked to pass on any of my stories, he would 'see me right' for a guinea or two. I somewhat prissily told him I couldn't do that as I was under contract not to do lineage.

"Gawd 'elp me," he said, "I've met the only honest reporter on the planet – it's a story in itself."

And he limped off to his decrepit Austin car, raised his trilby hat, bowed and drove off.

Our idols at this time were the reporters two or three years ahead of us, known in the trade as 'improvers'; senior status not being achieved until the age of 24. These included Peter Jones, who was headed for a career covering showbiz; George Dines, who could spin a joke better than anyone I've ever met, including the pro's, who had followed his father into sports writing; and a near-legendary figure called Peter O'Hanlon whose drunken adventures usually involved the pursuit of a 'gorgeous young sweetheart' – not excluding barmaids and grateful older women such as pub landladies.

Celebration after a Chapel meeting

We 'apprentices' looked on the union as another source of education. And the NUJ helped us out here with the occasional instructional weekend aimed at fostering union loyalty. The first I went on was a trip to Bristol, staying at Wills Hall, part of the university, in the august company of Michael Gabbert, Peter Michel (who'd joined the paper before me), Laurie Bloomfield (son of Bloomy) and Brian Northeast who worked on a weekly in Bognor but had been on the NCTJ course with me.

Five of us in a car built for four, and not a licence between us. We only stopped once on our drive westward, a nice pub on the outskirts of Salisbury, but this probably accounted for constant arguments about the best route to take.

However, we made up for the abstinence after taking up our rooms at Wills Hall, studies which were vacated by students during holiday-time. We were very good on the Saturday, attending every session, and arguing strenuously against any ideas put forward by the union hierarchy – just for the hell of it. Gabbert and Bloomfield made a point of demolishing any speaker who was in favour of the training course, with the rest of us joining in whenever we had the chance.

We did a round tour of the more famous pubs, the rugby fans' haunt, the Hatchet, in Denmark Street being a favourite, though we gave the old Mauretania a fair share of our charm as well.

"We definitely scored there," Peter Michel announced after we were politely asked to leave.

Later that night, Gabbert insisted on showing off his strength by carrying Brian Northeast up two flights of stairs at Wills Hall. And I retaliated by using a judo throw to toss Gabbert down to the next landing. Luckily he was too de-sensitised by alcohol to get hurt.

We were all very quiet on the Sunday afternoon drive back. All I recall was that we stopped for a drink in Salisbury, and then, for no reason anyone could recall later, we climbed a hill to see a lighthouse....in the middle of rural Wiltshire.

Chapter Seven
One Phone Between Three

After my probation period in Portsmouth, Mr Collings, who by now I casually referred to as 'Colly' (journalism being a profession where every single person was known by a nickname) asked for me to be transferred to Gosport where my local knowledge might be useful. I was to work with him and Ted Brett in the *Evening News'* old-fashioned, bow-windowed premises in the High Street, strategically placed opposite the main post office.

It was pretty cramped. There was a front office, staffed by Mike Foster and his girl assistant, with a door to the street and a long counter with an up-and-over flap for us to pass through. In a dimly-lit room at the back – we had to keep the light on almost all day – Colly, Ted and I shared a large table. We each had a typewriter – nicked from the Ark by that old matelot, Noah, said Ted – and there was one phone which sat on a small table in the corner.

A corridor at the back led to the sole toilet and in that passageway Ted and I kept our bikes. Colly had a car – a nice little runabout Morris, and he often gave Ted and me a lift.

The office was, of course, open to the public and the public made full use of that. Mike would stick a head round our door and ask if we were in to Mr or Mrs So-and-So and we would either show ourselves or ask him to take a note so we could call back. In return, one of us would fill in for him – selling a paper or filling out a form for the 'Hatched, Matched and Despatched' columns.

Messengers from head office would come over on the ferry at irregular intervals with paperwork for Mike – advertising proofs and so on – and would take back any copy we had for the editorial department. Anything like a scoop, of course, we would phone in to the copy-typists in Pompey. 'Hold the Front Page, Kitty!'

We were always busy. I learned that most of the work was diary-based – courts, council meetings, committee meetings, sports events including table tennis tournaments and so on.

So I soon found myself back at school, this time in the staff room to interview one of the teachers about a charity event. Barbara Thomson (French Lit.) greeted me warmly as did Jock Keast (Maths). I found myself chatting happily, asking how my sixth-form gang were getting on. Mr Hunt (Latin) walked in:

"Ah Jimpy...." he said (I'd put on a dismal, under-rehearsed attempt at a magic show for charity when in the Third Form – and ever after, he nicknamed me after the boy magician in a newspaper comic strip). "I suppose you smoke now," he added in his light, Irish brogue. I happily agreed, ready to accept a fag.

"Get 'em out then, bhoyo," he said, and he and Keast relieved me of two of my precious John Player's.

One major part of our job – which has mercifully now disappeared – was our coverage of funerals. Apart from the obvious newsworthy ones of local celebrities who might merit a fulsome obituary running to as much as a page, there were the funerals of all the little people – the working-class men and women who made up the bulk of the town of Gosport. They nearly always ran an announcement in the Deaths column of the paper and Colly would make a note in the diary so that we could cover the funeral. Usually this was the junior's job – and why should I miss out?

The drill was to arrive at the church, if there was to be a short service, stand at the door and take the names of anyone who came to pay their respects. On the other hand if there was to be a service at the graveside – the committal – usually at Gosport's huge cemetery on both sides of Ann's Hill Road, then I would have to go there and take down people's names as they arrived. Some of them would be expecting this and would hand over a printed visiting card.

I soon noticed that I would often see the same faces that I'd seen at the last funeral, or the one before that. Strange, I thought, they couldn't possibly be related to all these people. I mentioned this to Ted one day when I was typing out one of our interminable lists of mourners for the paper.

"Wondered when you'd spot that," he said cheerfully, "it happens everywhere. Some people just don't have enough to fill their day, so they become professional mourners, except they are not being paid....just there for something to do."

To give you a flavour of what it was like to be a small-town reporter, here's a typical day:

By some miracle I was in the office before Colly arrived:

"Ah, glad you're here," he said. "How's your French?"

"A-level – grammar poor, pronunciation not bad," I admitted.

"Good. There's a strange craft flying the French tricolour anchored just off the harbour ferry pontoon. Go and see if there's a story in it. I'd put you down to cover the open day on Foudroyant anyway, so you might as well do two birds with one stone. The old ship's now the home of the Girls Nautical Training Corps. They'll give you a decent lunch, by the way."

The Foudroyant was an old 'wooden wall', the ex-navy frigate HMS Trincomalee, built the day after Nelson's, so to speak.

Colly was right about the Frenchie: she had a mainmast and a ketch-style sail aft, and the central hull had two sort of outriggers either side. Today, with so many oversized trimarans all the style, she probably wouldn't look quite so strange.

Jerry, a young waterman I'd been at school with, was working off the ferry pontoon so I asked him to take me out to the stranger. I saw the name on the transom read Tohu Bohu, which I thought sounded a bit Polynesian.

"Ahoy, the yacht!" I hollered as we came alongside, and a bearded face appeared in the cockpit.

"*Je suis journaliste – puis-j'embarquer?*" I asked, and he leaned over to give me a hand on board.

"Best of British, mate," said Jerry as he shoved off, clearly thinking he'd never see me again this side of Shanghai.

Claude Genet, the skipper, led me into a surprisingly roomy cabin where his crew of four were tucking into a very British breakfast of bacon and eggs. Without preamble, one of them pushed a mug of strong black coffee towards me. I stayed with them for a cheerful hour, painfully explaining that I wanted to write a story about them for the local paper and gleaning that they were planning a three-year voyage round the world – in the craft they built themselves in the garden of Claude's house in Paris....

Idiots, I thought – but romantic idiots.

"'Tohu Bohu' means everything in a mess," Claude explained, and yes it was of Polynesian derivation.*

Out on deck, as I was thanking the brave Frenchmen and wishing them 'Bon voyage', I noticed that the girl cadets had started ferrying their guests out to Foudroyant, and I grabbed the chance to hail one of the boats to take me aboard. Up on the quarterdeck of the old wooden wall I found the open day was also being covered by my photographer mate Roy West, and I asked him to get a picture of Tohu Bohu and her crew while we had the chance.

Our piece duly appeared in the paper next day – "Makes quite a respectable page lead," said Colly.

Aboard Foudroyant we met the skipper, Captain Spalding, ex-navy, a man not to be confused with the Groucho Marx character, as in 'Hooray for Captain Spalding the African explorer', which Roy kept

---

* In later life I discovered that 'Claude Genet' is the name of a famous champagne – and that 'Tohu Bohu' is not Polynesian but comes from the book of Genesis and means 'formless or chaotic'. Ah well, I wasn't the first journalist to be taken for a ride by a matelot with a sense of humour and, as Shakespeare, said "That's been going on since Noah was a sailor."

singing *sotto voce* as we toured the ship with the Lord Mayor and Mayoress of Portsmouth.

The lassies of the Girls Nautical Training Society used to spend a week pretending to be foremast jacks in Nelson's navy – even to sleeping in hammocks slung in the fo'csle with the regulation 14 inches between each body. I did wonder whether they used lower deck language as well....but didn't fancy asking.

Then we all had a chicken salad lunch in the great stern cabin, accompanied by a glass of decent chilled white wine, and followed by traditional strawberries and cream. I stopped off at the office to type out my two stories and then hopped on a bus to Brockhurst Road and Podd's House Day Nursery, where they were celebrating their anniversary.

The very-matronly head of the businesss took me under her wing and introduced Nurse Betty McAnulty who was to look after me, kindly explaining what was on the programme and who was who. (How can I still remember her name? Easy, I see the lovely Betty every Sunday in church. Small town, Gosport). The children presented their own Coronation show – with a tiny Queen Elizabeth and her own Prince Philip. I was amazed and vastly entertained by these tiny singers and dancers. They all had surprisingly loud voices, though well on the shrill side. They danced energetically like little whirling dervishes and hurled themselves into a frenzied finale, when about 100 of them rushed at the audience showering the Mums in a storm of rose petals – while a yelling splinter group climbed all over me and bore me to my knees. Then we all had strawberries and cream (again) for tea.

At Gosport, each reporter had a key to the office so that we could get in after hours. Fixed to the wall was a small box where non-urgent copy was placed for the next messenger to pick up. We also had a private arrangement with our naval correspondent, Howard Fairclough, known as Fairy. He lived in quiet Carlton Road, the other side of St George's Barracks – sometimes army, sometimes navy – and we often used to drop off overnight copy for him to deliver to head office. Alternatively, we had special envelopes marked 'Urgent Mail' and 'Photos Do Not Bend' which we could use to post copy – the last pick-up from the main post office was (unbelievable today) not until 2am.

The placing of our High Street office was very handy. Every Saturday, after the usual morning calls, Colly would lead us across the street to the Swiss Café for coffee. This was a regular meeting place for *hoi poloi* of the town – councillors, lawyers, business men and women, ladies that ran the local organisations and charities, and so on – and we were effectively flying the flag.

Unless there was a pressing job on the diary, we lingered over coffee for about an hour.

I have never seen anyone consume as much sugar as Colly managed to get into a cup of coffee – and he usually had four cups in the course of the morning. The only person who took this phenomenon in her stride was the waitress – known to one and all as 'Cash and Carry Connie'. Ted once revealed to me that Michael Gabbert, during his stint in Gosport, had had a fling with her. I can't say I blamed him.

Colly, Ted and local paper journalism combined to change me dramatically. I'd already realised that a reporter's job was actually very different from real life. Here was a profession that admired enterprise above all things, rather like the Royal Navy. It was the chief reason why the earlier in life you began, the better you would be.

One day Colly asked me if I'd ever flown in a plane, and I confessed that I had not.

"Ah you'll probably find this interesting," he said, shoving a pamphlet across the desk. A bunch of keen enthusiasts at HMS Daedalus, home of the Royal Navy Fleet Air Arm at Lee-on-the-Solent, were setting up a Glider Club and were inviting the *Evening News* to send a reporter along for a flight.

"Do you fancy a flip in a glider?" Colly asked. "Ted and I can't go because we're both married, you see. But you are still single, so you're the obvious candidate," he added with typical graveyard humour.

I was scared at the very idea of going up in the air with no engine, but there was no way I was going to turn down the challenge. The following Saturday I was met outside a hangar at Daedalus by a guy in his fifties – a retired navy flyer. He took me out to a weird-looking machine sitting on the runway, leaning over so that one wing was touching the grass verge. Part of the reason it looked so strange was the propellor – there wasn't one.

We climbed in and I sat just behind him. Some crewmen fitted us up with a towline attached to the glider's nose. There was a slight tug and the towing aircraft, a light single-engined plane, took off and pulled us up into the blue sky. There was a continuous shushing noise of air moving over our glider, which abruptly stopped as the towline was dropped. We were some thousand feet up, I suppose, and the ground, spread out like a map, tilted slightly every time we made one of our slow, curving turns.

"You okay?" the pilot asked. I said I was, and managed to squeak out something about the wonderful view. As I said it, the wonderful view disappeared and I found I was looking out at empty space. This phenomenon was accompanied by a sudden lurch as the glider dropped – it felt to me like hundreds of feet – over the sea, a flat ultramarine expanse stretching widely east and west.

"Always does that," said the pilot matter-of-factly. "Change of temperature I think."

I didn't like the 'think' bit – I'd rather have a little more certainty about this trip, thanks.

But I was really enjoying the cruise as we came in over the cliffs. I could appreciate how high we were by how much land there was in every direction. Eventually the runway was just ahead and we came rushing down out of the sky to land.

"Fancy another trip?"

"Yes, please....I think...."

And round we went again. This time I was ready for the slight jolt of the towline coming off. And I could see we were now quite a lot higher as we cruised, spiralling slowly downward. Suddenly the pilot dipped the nose, the plane dived forward, picking up speed and then the ground strangely seemed to come up from behind me and rolled over my head, while my stomach turned a somersault. I was gasping for air as we levelled out.

The pilot had just performed a backward roll. He grinned at me: "How was that then?"

"Bloody marvellous," I lied, idiot that I was, because he laughed and said:

"Let's do it again then...." and round we went and once more I had to wait for my stomach to catch up. But yes, it was exhilarating – and I said so in my piece for the paper.

Part of my job was to write a lengthy column of youth notes for our weekly, *The Hampshire Telegraph*. Michael Gabbert had started it as *Spotlight on Youth by Apollo*. At least he looked like an Apollo with his big weightlifter's frame and his blond hair. Not surprisingly there are hardly any photos of me at this age – in fact the only one was a photo taken of the cast of *A Midsummer's Night Dream* (which the sixth form had put on in my last summer at school). This picture makes me look rather like a wistful romantic poet about to do himself in. But I don't think *Youth Notes by Shelley* would have cut it. In those days, of course, everyone had these fancy pen-names: the paper never let you have your own name as a by-line in case you became famous and demanded more money.

Apart from picking up news and gossip from the many youth

clubs in town, I met the town's Youth Officer once a week to catch up on any initiatives by the borough council. I also attended youth committees, which led me to meet town worthies such as the Mayor and aldermen, such worthies as Bob Nobes, the Labour man, or Charlie Osborn, the Tory leader. Among the meetings I attended was the Gosport Sea Cadet Committee – and to my astonishment I was encouraged to put forward the 'youth view' on various topics.

In this way I came to be on regular chatting terms with important local figures (it's a navy town, remember) such as Admiral Agnew and Admiral Grace or, perhaps more importantly, their wives. The admirals were determined to build a new meeting place for the cadets in a spare corner of St Vincent, the navy training establishment for new recruits where, on passing-out parade, the most successful young seaman stood – totally unsupported – at the top of the rigging of the huge mast that towered over the town. He was known as the Button Boy, because he only had a button to stand on.

With the important people in the town apparently taking me seriously, and the influence of my contemporaries like Peter Michel, Laurie Bloomfield and Michael Gabbert, I began to develop the beginning of a personality. We took ourselves very seriously sometimes, always referring to each other as 'Old Boy'. As in the expression 'Christoleboy' to convey surprise or astonishment....

Nancy was quick to notice the difference. I found it much easier to talk to her. Her mother was a colleague of Dr Reginald Bennett at Knowle mental hospital near Fareham and I quite often met him at her home, where he regarded me as a fellow guest. He was also the MP for Gosport and Fareham, so he treated me as a source of information (or he pretended to) and went out of his way to acknowledge me at any function where we met.

Early on I decided a motorbike would be handy and I bought a secondhand BSA 250cc from a young man who lived next door to my Gran. This was practically a vintage machine – it dated from 1933 or thereabouts – with those funny little cables on the handlebars to advance or retard the ignition, whatever that did. It had originally been fitted with a hand gear-change on the petrol tank, but some later owner had added a foot change. I paid a whacking £20 for this bike.

Ted clearly didn't think much of my bargain, but he came up trumps by handing over some of his old motorbike gear – big gauntlets and a waterproof coat – and gave me some help getting the hang of the thing. No-one was very impressed by my bike –

except one of my schoolmates, Graeme Matthews, who I gave a pillion ride along the seafront, totally illegally, of course, since I had no L-plates and no licence.

Despite all the stuff I'd read about bikes in *Boy's Own Paper*, I was mechanically illiterate. I knew how to turn on the petrol, make sure the bike was in neutral, kick down on the pedal to start her up, then pull in the clutch, find first gear with my right foot, then slowly let out the clutch to move off, going through the gears. I kept wondering why, when I stopped in top gear, the damn thing wouldn't start again, but always stalled. No-one had told me you had to start off in first and go through the gears every time. Sounds stupid, but there it was. I'd get to the end of the road, brake and stop....and then have to push it back home and start again. Until some kind rider stopped alongside and, after a short discussion, let me into the big secret. I didn't dare tell Ted.

In fact the only time I used the bike was to get to Stubbington on Wednesdays for my district calls. I can tell you I was pretty proud of having my own territory. As far as this village was concerned, I was the eyes and ears of the world. Colly gave me a list of village leaders to call on – among them, Mrs Ann Dale, local councillor; the vicar, the Rev H A Eyton-Jones; and Mrs King, a charming lady who knew everyone. The list had been compiled by many young reporters going back into the mists of time – some of the people had long ago passed on. There was also an old boy who was Stubbington's oldest cricketer – a wicked spin bowler who was still skittling them out well into his nineties and long after I'd married and brought up a family. He was an absolute mine of information on anything relating to sport.

Mrs Dale filled columns of village news for me (she became popular enough in the area to have a school named after her). The vicar, an Oxford rowing blue who wangled his way into being the official Chaplain to Cowes Week, was a colourful source in his own right. He rarely gave me a story that wasn't connected with fund-raising, money being his principal interest in life.

There were two highlights of my career as Chronicler of Stubbington – the first was on June 2, 1953 when I covered the Coronation of Queen Elizabeth II. A very big deal in our neck of the woods, because of the Coronation Fleet Review just offshore in the Solent. Navies from all over the world contributed ships on a scale that has never been matched. On Coronation Day I clattered up to the village green on my elderly BSA, a series of horrific exhaust blasts drowning out the national anthem being played by a local band. There was a crowd of people in rainwear, kids damply waving sodden little flags on sticks, a groaning loudspeaker system relaying the Rev Eyton-Jones's loyal oration....and a brave march-past of Scouts, Guides and, of course, the Stubbington Covenanters (remember the great sporting footballers?). Things vastly improved when we all repaired to the village pub, when we were all more than happy to drink a toast to our radiant young queen.

Eyton-Jones' saving grace was that he was deeply interested in the village's original church, Crofton Old Church. The place was crumbling away, hardly ever used for services, and was expected to be allowed to fall into ruin, but Eyton-Jones said it showed definite signs of Saxon origins and I took a polite interest when he showed me his research notes.

Now the *Evening News* carried every day on Page 2, a *By the Way* column – a rag-bag of pieces of 'interesting' non-news. All reporters were expected to contribute to this and the chief sub used to phone backsliders: "Ah Mr Bull, we haven't had a *Way* par (that's what we called them) from you for some time now. Perhaps you'd like to put that right."

When I mentioned this in the pub, Michael Gabbert said: "Do what the rest of us do – make something up."

"Such as?"

"Let's see....'Over the sweltering weekend, girl strawberry-pickers toiling in the fields of south-east Hampshire....were trying to cool off by stripping to the waist. An incident that did not go unnoticed by passing drivers.'"

Look back through the files of the popular press and you will see a paragraph like that every early June – phoned in by one or other of us, regular as the first cuckoo, year in, year out. Enterprise, see?

We were also encouraged to contribute articles of historic or environmental interest – up to 1,000 words, for which the editor paid half-a-guinea. More importantly, these pieces carried your own true by-line. So the first time my by-line appeared in print was on Page 2 – 'When Samuel Pepys rode over to Crofton,' by John Bull. I hope my humble contribution all those years ago helped to stimulate interest in the old place: in recent years it has been extensively restored and is well used for special services.

By early summer we were entering the season of outdoor events, including many local shows. When the Fareham and Hants Farmers' Club Show came round, Colly lent me to the Fareham reporter Reg Betts for the day to help out. By happy chance the showground was just to the north of Fareham, only a short walk from Nancy's home.

Mind you, it meant a lot of dreary drudgery in the Press tent (there were reporters from all over south Hampshire, including the

Hampshire Chronicle, Southern Daily Echo and the trade weeklies with an interest in farming. It was one the more prominent shows in the south – in an earlier year, one of these shows had caused a great deal of embarrassment to the *Evening News* for the infamous headline, on the front page lead:

Queen's success at Petworth Show
First prize for Windsor cow

I heard that copies of the *News* (price 2d) were being flogged around the pubs for two shillings a time before anyone at head office noticed the clanger.

Back to the Fareham show – Reg and I, and our-man-in-Winchester Bob Gamble, slogged away typing great lists of winners in hundreds of classes, with a carbon and a second sheet of paper in the machine to make a copy (known in the trade as a black) for our weekly paper to carry on Friday. Any big results like the Champion Show Bull were phoned through to the copytakers at Stanhope Road. Around this point, the boredom was eased by the opening of the refreshment tent – and the offer of free beer for the Press.

I'm just finishing a refreshing pint of Badger when John Prentice, our Fareham office manager (there to sell papers with results stamped into the Stop Press column alongside the latest racing results), strolls up.

"There's a nice little filly wandering around looking for you," he says, loud enough for everyone to notice. In my ear he adds: "I sent her to the flower show marquee."

There's Nancy, taking in the scent of an impressive display of roses. I think my heart actually skips several beats as she turns – and smiles at me. Absolute silence in the tent. Maybe they all disappeared.

"Please move away from the roses," I whisper. "You're making them look dowdy."

(I'd like a fiver for every time I've used that line in my life – but truly, that was its first and best outing).

She poked me in the ribs and then gave me a peck on the cheek. I know she came to help Reg and me with the results in the Press tent, but any memory of that was lost in the bliss of first love.

That evening I took Nancy to the pictures and for the first time

I was bold enough to put my arm around her and hug her close to me as we walked down the lane into town. The film, in case you wonder, was *Genevieve* with John Gregson, a romantic comedy with the unforgettable show-stopping bit where Kay Kendall plays a jazz number on the trumpet.

Otherwise the show was stolen by Genevieve (played by a vintage Darracq) and another vintage motor-car, in the London-to-Brighton car run. The score was a masterpiece of light music by Larry Adler and played largely on his harmonica: there was a different theme for each car. The other stars were Kenneth More and Dinah Sheridan.

The summer of 1952 duly segued into another glorious autumn. Reporting, however, became a job rather than a crusade as the pressure of mundane diary jobs tended to limit chances of finding the good, offbeat story. And when we did, Colly usually covered it himself – for example a strike at Gosport's Fleetlands naval aircraft repair yard which attracted national press and radio coverage.

One afternoon I was alone in the office, probably a Wednesday as early closing day meant Foster and his office girl went home at 1pm.

The phone rang: "Gabbert here, old boy. If a little bird tells you there's been a plane crash on your patch, Johnjo, don't worry, it's all in hand. I've done a par for the Stop Press, and a full story for tomorrow. Cheers, Old Boy."

See what I mean about Enterprise? Thank you, Michael. Just what I didn't need.

As far as the work went I learned how to cover court – being introduced to the arcane mysteries of English law (which differs distinctly from the Scottish system) and, of course, we covered inquests. This was a whole different education in itself: this was the real world way beyond textbook fantasies.

I still feel the shock of discovering how many girls died in botched backstreet abortions. Enough to make you sit up and take notice, though it was never on the scale that I encountered when I later went to work in South London where, at my local coroner's court, they were fishing pregnant suicides out of the Thames at the rate of one a week. What a terrible waste of lives. Not many journalists, policemen or coroner's officers were anti-abortion. Maybe it isn't the best thing, but making it legal was probably the most humane advance since my youth. That and the Pill of course.

The courts were equally amazing as the scales dropped daily from my eyes: a never-ending parade of the desperate stepping up to the dock. We *Evening News* reporters had to work at speed, too. We kept stock of copy paper in the drawer of our Press table.

Every half hour or so, a copy boy came from the office to take back any stories we had already written up. It was the proud boast of your skilled court reporter that he'd finish writing up a case before the magistrates came back to announce the verdict and pronounce sentence.

I recall being entranced by the antique language. Here's a sample dialogue from the Clerk to the Court, a law officer whose job was to advise magistrates and also defendants:

Clerk to defendant: "You are here today because it is said that you did – to the annoyance of our Sovereign Lady Queen Elizabeth II – lewdly, openly and deliberately expose your person with an intent to insult a female. Do you plead guilty or not guilty?"

Honestly I'm not making this up – the language was not only archaic, it was beautiful in a rhythmic sort of way. I wouldn't be surprised to learn that it had all been written by Tyndale, the great translator of the English Bible.

Everyone appearing in the dock was supposed innocent until proved guilty. If he had a record, no-one was allowed to mention it until he'd been found guilty. But there were ways round the system....

Picture a sad-looking middle-aged man in a crumpled suit in the dock, charged with indecency in a public place. And another middle-aged man in a crumpled suit, DC Faircop, takes the stand, and swears to tell the truth 'So help me God.'

"Your Worships – I saw the accused enter the gents' public toilet in the Guildhall Square, and I followed him inside. I noticed that one of the cubicles was closed. I then entered an adjoining cubicle and by standing on the toilet seat was able to look over the partition into the cubicle next door. I saw the accused was accompanied by a young sailor in a compromising attitude. I said: 'What are you doing in there?'

"The defendant replied (here Faircop pauses and riffles through the pages of his notebook) 'Oh hello Mr Faircop....'"

The constable might just as well have said: "This bloke's got a record as long as your arm."

The magistrate purses his lips, gives Faircop a long, sad look, sniffs, and says:

"Thank you Detective Constable, you may step down." And then he also sends the defendant down – for three months.

This is the magistrates court, the basic starting-point for all criminal jurisdiction. With few exceptions all cases start in the magistrate courts, sometimes known as courts of summary jurisdiction, or petty sessions. They cover everything from murder to an application for a licence to sell booze at the village hall New Year's Eve dance.

In my early days these were the most likely places for young reporters to cut their teeth before moving up, say, to Quarter Sessions, or even Assizes – the really serious, most ceremonial, most archaic and dramatic of scenarios. A lot of changes have occurred since my teeth-cutting days, mostly for the better. However we do miss some of the theatre of it all. See a long line of begowned and bewigged judges marching in colourful array into the Great Hall at Winchester for the start of the Assizes, and you begin to grasp the full meaning of the 'panoply' of the law.

Watch nervously as a grim-faced judge solemnly dons his black cap and tells the poor bugger literally shivering in the dock: "You will be taken to a place of execution where you will be hanged by the neck until you are dead...." I once saw a young reporter faint clean away.

And up to now I've been talking about criminal courts. Working alongside were the civil proceedings, usually in the county court. Most big towns had them in my early days, complete with circuit judges – not people to mess with.

As a newcomer I was entrusted with the Juvenile Court coverage, though I ran into a snag on the first day. I was just settling in at the Press table when a police officer – an inspector in full uniform – came over.

"How old are you, son?" he asks.

"I'm 17."

"Ah – well I'm afraid you can't stay here. No-one under the age of 18 is allowed in the Juvenile Court."

"But I'm from the Evening News – to report on the cases."

"Sorry, but it is the law, you know."

At this point the court Clerk intervenes:

"You raise a good point, Inspector, but in fact, there is nothing to prevent this young man from doing his job. We have no power to stop him. Besides....I don't know how you feel, but I don't relish reading 'Court bid to silence the Press' in the morning papers...."

The inspector hummed and hawed a bit: clearly he and the clerk were not the best of chums. But he took his seat and I got on with the job.

Indeed this was a bit of an eye-opener for me – rightly or wrongly, fair or unfair, it dawned on me that journalists were in a very privileged position. The power of the Press wasn't just an idle, throwaway line: it could carry real clout.

For us reporters, lawyers, cops, probation officers and the amazing number of people who just popped in to watch, the court proceedings were an endless theatrical performance. There was ceremony, drama, and often sheer knockabout comedy on the bill. You learn a bit about human nature, too. For instance, my days in the Juvenile Court, where the children involved could not be identified, of course, taught me that males and females reacted very differently. As a general rule, boys tended to hold up me 'and for that one, Guv' when confronted with their guilt; whereas girls tended to go on blustering 'I never done nuffink mister' in the face of the most blindingly obvious evidence.

We once listened to a dapper little man in the dock explaining why he should be allowed bail until his case was heard at Quarter Sessions. He was accused of maliciously wounding his wife by breaking a bottle over her head. He sobbed as he described how he came to do it....he loved her, you see. He unrolled a story of years of looking after his beloved Sarah, he worshipped the ground she walked on. His only regret was that they had never been able to have a child....He would do anything to cancel out that stupid, once in a lifetime unlucky blow....she was coming out of hospital later that day, he would beg her forgiveness....

The public was clearly moved by his tale. The magistrates, too, seemed impressed; there would be a brief adjournment.

I was scribbling away with the story; the other *News* reporter and also the hard-bitten freelance, Dennis Tressider, agreed with me. This was a rare exception to the rule – this chap was really a decent fellow who deserved a break.

The magistrates returned and the chairman told the husband in the dock that they were going to take the unusual step of granting bail in such a serious case. There were nods of approval, even from the policemen in court.

That evening this loving husband drove to the hospital and, as his wife walked over to the car, he revved up and ran her over. She wasn't expected to live – he was charged with attempted murder.

Now we journalists rarely get it that wrong – but with people, you can never really be sure.

On the lighter side there was the sheer joy of watching a good advocate go about his business. One of the best was Gosport solicitor Archie Kingswell. A big man with a open, friendly face, Archie was a joy to see in action. He had a trick of chewing his tongue, which I believe was his way of giving himself time to think. Not that he needed too much of that – he was one of the quickest thinkers in the game.

One day at Gosport magistrates court Archie was in full flood pleading mitigation for his defendant, when a shrill scream came from the direction of the cells.

"No doubt someone helping the police with their enquiries," Archie said. "Now as I was saying...." to a courtroom laughing its socks off.

He wasn't one to give up too easily either. He was involved in a case of alleged breach of public decency at Gosport's popular White Hart pub. A police inspector and two constables gave evidence that on a Sunday evening they were in the pub and heard a sailor on the microphone singing "a notorious song with indecent lyrics", to whit *Sweet Violets*.

"Eh? What indecent lyrics? Is there something I don't know?" I asked myself – and so, I imagine, did everyone else in the court. *Sweet Violets* was an old Victorian song but in 1951 had shot to number three in the American charts when it was recorded by Dinah Shore. The lyrics were suggestive, sure, but nothing was actually expressed. However the landlord, Major Oberst, was found guilty and fined £5.

Nearly a year later the case went to appeal in London – in the Queen's Bench division before the Lord Chief Justice, Lord Goddard, no less, sitting with Mr Justice Omerod and Mr Justice Gorman. The facts of the *Sweet Violets'* outrage to decency on a Sunday evening prompted lively discussion – especially when it was said that the entertainment was led by a comic dressed as a parson in a dog collar....

"Seems very appropriate to the day," commented Lord Goddard to considerable laughter in court. Their Honours found a sensible way of quashing the case – on the grounds that it should never have been brought by the police, but by the licensing authority, Gosport Borough Council.

I hope the gallant major got his fiver back – plus his legal costs.

Rightly or wrongly, those of us who spent a great deal of our time covering the various types of law courts often found them very similar to the music hall. The stars were the sharp-tongued judges or magistrates and sometimes a serial offender would have a well-worn act that the audience – lawyers, police, press, magistrates – relied on to break up the awful monotony of the minor cases. Most courts also had a hard core of men and women who had nothing better to do with their days except take advantage of this endless, free entertainment.

Portsmouth's County (civil) Court was noted for a judge who thought he had a gift for stand-up and who would often direct one of his *bon mots* in the direction of the Press box, in case you didn't get the joke. Then you would slip out of the room and phone a piece straight in to the copy-takers. Here's one of mine that made the main edition.

Barrister: Your Honour, the bedroom in question is 9ft across and 31ft in length.

Judge: More like a rifle gallery then.

(Laughter in court).

There were some apocryphal stories knocking around about magistrates, too. One of them featured a well-known Hampshire titled lady, let's call her Lady Erica, who is sitting next to the presiding chairman, let's say Admiral Sir Timothy, at Fareham magistrates court.

A young girl witness is being pressed by the prosecuting police inspector to tell the court what the accused said to her just before the alleged indecent assault. After a bit of cajoling, and a little bullying, the girl agrees to write it down – and her note is passed first to the defendant in the box, then to his solicitor, then up to the bench.

Now it is a rather warm, summer afternoon, and the admiral, after a decent lunch at the Red Lion, has nodded off, his eyes masked behind his specs. The clerk hands the note to Lady Erica who glances at it, digs the admiral in the ribs and slips the note into his hand.

He clears his throat, coughs and reads: "Do you fuck?"

Red-faced, he turns to Lady Erica and in a hoarse whisper the courtroom is not meant to hear demands: "Have you taken leave of your senses, Madam?"

More antique solemnity came my way when Colly asked me to pop over to Portsmouth to cover a Royal Navy court martial.

"There'll be other reporters there who will show you the ropes, so don't worry about it. Just do what they do." In other words, the typical learn-on-the job system that newspapers went in for.

So I arrived at Nelson's old flagship HMS Victory, permanently in dry dock in Portsmouth Dockyard but still, amazingly, in commission as a warship – which indeed, with charming naval etiquette, she still is today.

The set-up and rules for the court martial – in the great stern cabin of the ship – were not much changed from Nelson's day either. It was presided over by an admiral in gleaming full fig dripping gold braid, flanked by senior officers and a clerk sitting behind a long table on which, in the trial of a commissioned officer, was laid his own ceremonial sword. This was used as a pointer to the verdict. If the sword pointed towards the defendant it meant guilty – if the other way round, he was cleared. At least that's what they told me though I never actually saw it done.

The prosecuting officer had a small table on one side of the cabin: on the other side, facing him, sat another officer known as the Accused's Friend. Dennis Tressider, one of the Pompey freelances, was already sitting at the Press table, set up at the back of the courtroom. There was one other chair – empty.

One of the officers leaned over and whispered something to the admiral. The admiral made a dismissive gesture.

"Oh, no...." he boomed. "Can't start yet, old Bennett's not here. Got to wait for Bennett, what?"

Tressider whispered to me: "You'll love this. They're waiting for Bennett of the *Times*....he must be nearly 90."

A little later there was a bit of confusion at the narrow doorway to the great cabin. To my amazement the presiding admiral got down from his seat and hurried over to the door.

The old chap coming in – it could only be the legendary Bennett – gave a loud chuckle and stuck out his hand, which the admiral shook warmly.

"How are you, you old devil?" he said.

"Fine, fine, Algy," said Bennett.

Tress leaned over to me: "You gotta remember old Bennett's been a naval correspondent most of his life. He knew all of today's gold braid when they were Snotties, y'know, midshipmen. They all love him."

"Well we must have a chat later," said the admiral and, resuming his customary Captain Bligh look, returned to the president's chair.

The newcomer came and sat next to me. "Bennett of the *Times*," he said in a stage whisper that could be heard by everyone in the cabin.

"Bull, *Pompey News*," I whispered to him.

He was, naturally, a mine of information. What he didn't know about the complex rules of Royal Navy justice wasn't worth knowing. He steered me and other reporters through some tricky waters.

One story in our weekly paper *Hampshire Telegraph and Naval Chronicle* (to give it its full title at that time) was headlined :

Officer Hated the Service

It featured a young sub-lieutenant who had absented himself from his duty station for an afternoon and a night. According to his defence, an officer known as 'the accused's friend,' he had gone home because he was unhappy with the Royal Navy. He was quoted as saying he got fed up with his fellow officers making fun of him because of his working-class Yorkshire accent.

The court found he was guilty of being absent without leave, but instead of having his wish to leave the Royal Navy granted, he was simply sentenced to loss of seniority. I got the impression they were not anxious to lose people, maybe something to do with the Cold War? Or, being admirals, they needed to keep as many ranks filled to justify their own existence....Not for me to say, is it?

Because here's another case where they appear to have leaned over backwards to keep a particular cook on board for some years. Maybe he was a good cook.

He was up for disobeying an order from a PO – and wounding him. The accused's friend said the cook was one of eight children. He couldn't recall his father ever working, though his mother was a cleaner. He wanted to be a boxer, but his mother objected and he joined the navy. He had clocked up a number of offences of being absent without leave and had been sentenced to several terms of detention.

"However," said the officer, "apart from his failure to respect discipline, his character is good."

The cook was sentenced to 18 months' detention and dismissed the service. My headline would have been:

The One That Got Away

But then nobody asked me.

Chapter Eight
A Handful of Stars

The summer of 1953 was just another of those dreary, drizzly Fifties summers. Things did pick up a bit towards the end of August and we had a glorious burst of warm weather. Nancy and I spent lazy afternoons on our special bit of beach at Hill Head, or more correctly Meon Shore, where Hampshire's River Meon flows down from Titchfield to the sea. It was a magical place with a grassy spot just off the shingle beach with three or four lovely pine trees bringing some shade.

I recall a blue swimsuit that showed off her slim curves, her shapely limbs and her fresh peachy complexion. Her arms were sweetly around my neck, and her body warmly close. Remember this was the closest I'd ever been to a live girl.

We took advantage of warm evenings to take walks along the seafront. Lee Tower was a favourite place – we'd get the bus there from her home in Fareham and then go for a walk. We used to sit on a handy bench on the sea side of the tower and listen to the music from the dance-hall. The local resident band, The Gosporteers, had a fondness for George Shearing, so we were often serenaded by *September in the Rain* or *I'll Remember April*.

We always meant to get that last bus back – but I don't recall that we ever made it. So we used to walk back to Fareham, a good five miles along empty country lanes, discussing art and love, poetry and love, my job – her student days – and love. Frankie Laine's hit *Walking my Baby Back Home*: that's what we'd sing. Of course, having seen Nancy to her front door, or more likely the wide oak tree outside her front garden for a long, last embrace, I then had to stroll, happy, another five miles home. Love, see.

One night, to my annoyance, when I called for her I found she had a schoolfriend with her. I knew Mary Grigg because she came from a family of churchgoers and one Christmas our gang had pushed her around on a mobile organ, carol-singing in the streets and raising money for church charities. I was less than pleased to see her. Nancy took me to one side and said: "I could hardly tell her to go away – we've been friends for years."

It was decided that the three of us would go to the beach for a swim – then Nancy would stay overnight with Mary, who lived in Gosport fairly near my home.

51

So the three of us went swimming at Stokes Bay. We had a dip as the last rays of the sun lit the flat calm sea, and then went to the Village Home pub for a drink. Fortified by the booze, and armed with a miniature malt whisky bought over the bar, we headed back to the shore. We walked to Gilkicker, a lonely spot with an old fort right on the shingle beach. Coming back, Mary said it was getting late, time to go home.

Nancy, reluctant to let the mood go, said: "Hey why don't we have a last swim? Even better, why don't we make it skinny-dipping."

Bold hussies these two. Well, I was definitely not going to miss out on this. We stripped off, the girls strangely moving a bit away from me, presumably from modesty. Having less on that I had, they were quicker to plunge into the sea and start splashing water over each other.

The sea is warm milk, and up above the thousands of stars are twinkling in a velvet, moonless sky, all brilliantly mirrored in the flat surface of the Solent.

I swim about a bit, cherishing the all-over thrill of being naked in the sea. I scoop up water to splash over my head, releasing a glittering handful of stars....

Hey, what....?

I slosh up more water and a stream of luminous scales runs down my arm, I see my chest is covered in long threads of silver. On the surface, long trails of sparkles stretch away in all directions.

I shout to the girls and wave my glowing arms about.

Nancy and Mary suddenly realise their hair is a glowing halo of starshine – they shriek, scrabbling through the water, squealing, and trying to brush the scales off.

Picture the scene....two 'volumptuous' maidens, their young, supple bodies outlined in silver....like some Biblical Old Master leaping suddenly to life. I'm surprised I didn't swoon clean away.

The girls reach the beach and run for their towels. With perfect timing a car turns off the road and a pair of powerful headlights sweep the scene. The girls wrapped in their towels drop flat on the shingle, shrieking for me "do something, you idiot."

Like what? I pick up my own towel, walk gingerly over the stones and offer to give them a rub down.

"Go away," hollers Mary, struggling into her pants and bra, still highlighted by the headlights of the – no doubt fascinated – driver who maybe thought he'd stumbled on a pair of angels taking an evening dip.

I walked them both back to Mary's house where Nancy would stay the night. And then I walked home, sadly realising I couldn't tell anyone the story. If I wanted to keep my girlfriend, that is.

Incidentally, Mary had a trainee medical technician's job in Gosport, but when she heard that I earned some £4 a week as a trainee journo, she started writing to local papers for a job, eventually striking lucky with a weekly paper called the *Hants and Sussex Gazette* – widely known among its readers as *The Squeaker* – based in Petersfield.

Now in those days that corner of Hampshire and West Sussex was a short train or car ride from London and therefore very popular with an arty-crafty ménage of painters, poets, writers and actors. Names from the film world that often figured in the columns of *The Squeaker* included Mai Zetterling, the diminutive Swedish actress, and Alec Guinness, whose latest starring roles at this time were in *The Lavender Hill Mob* and *The Man in the White Suit*. Novelist Nevil Shute had lived nearby and was a great friend of Flora Twort, who ran the secondhand bookshop in The Square at Petersfield.

Mary was pretty soon rubbing shoulders with the stars, along with her editor boss Ray Barwick and her fellow cub reporter John Dodd. They may have rubbed shoulders with the glamour, but I have to tell you that their editorial suite at *The Squeaker* was at the back of the company's printing shop; a draughty, leaky shack with an earth floor. The *News* finally bought out *The Squeaker* in the late Fifties and Ray, never in the best of health since being a wartime prisoner of the Japanese, found a berth on the *Southern Daily Echo* in Southampton. Mary, after a spell as a Fleet Street columnist on the ill-fated *News Chronicle*, became a leading light in Amnesty International, and John Dodd a feature writer on the *Sun*. You couldn't say *The Squeaker* didn't foster talent.

Chapter Nine
Gott Knows Yer

In those days, there was one reason that most young couples got married rather hastily. Mike Gabbert was first, having got his girlfriend 'into trouble', and other friends of mine found themselves in the same jam. Nancy, too, reported that a couple of girls, old chums of hers, were going down what she called 'the natural path.' I was 18, she was six months younger – a bit young to settle down, we both agreed. The cooler autumn nights were a help: we probably wouldn't have survived sex-free, so to speak, if the Indian summer had gone on a bit.

Autumn was romantic enough. We'd go for long walks from her home, through a glorious wide field with a footpath through the middle, into an infinity of dark pines, stark against the setting sun. We walked and we talked. I can still picture the afterglow from a crimson sunset adding a faint, dark blush to her face, turned happily towards me.

I suppose one of the things that saved us was our nervousness about actual sex. We *talked* about it a lot, but kissing and cuddling was all it came to. We walked many miles: across some of the most beautiful countryside and along the crest of Portsdown Hill to Fort Nelson, looking down on the glitter of lights coming on in Pompey far below.

Towards the end of October we started looking for glowworms. Most people have probably never seen one. But as it happened I was used to them, because my father – a Wiltshire country lad – was field-savvy: he loved to pile up his compost heap at the end of summer, and then on the dark nights of October and November, before it became really cold, these strange creatures would turn their little lights on, to the delight of this small boy.

In those days, through the maturing (rotting) countryside, dying leaves everywhere around the footpath at the fields' edge, glowworms in the wild were easy to spot.

We didn't meet every night, of course. Sometimes I had jobs – a dinner-dance, a council meeting, or a youth club event to cover. Nancy had art college commitments. And traditionally I was expected to spend Saturday night with my old friends Dave and Les, my mates from our wartime days as Bomb Alley Kids. We used to go to Lee Tower for a glass or two of lager. Sometimes we wandered into the dancing in the ballroom, but this was not really to our taste: we were there to look at the girls and prop up the bar. The dance-floor was always packed: Lee Tower was the only proper dance-hall in town – and the whole town turned out on a Saturday night.

Lee Tower

We chatted to other people we knew, but mainly we spoke about the work we did. Dave was an apprentice bricklayer – he used to take me out to see houses that he was working on. A bit more substantial than writing stories for a newspaper, I told him. Les worked in the bar of the Isle of Wight paddle steamers, then run by British Rail, and dreamed of getting a steward's berth on an ocean liner, to see a bit of the world. He never did, though: Les died ludicrously young – and it seemed unfair after having survived the bombs.

The last bus left Lee Tower at about 11pm. But we hadn't finished our night out. We stayed on the bus all the way to the ferry and then walked back up the High Street and turned into Bemister's Lane. About halfway down this notorious old alley was a café. It was usually still busy at this time. A handpainted sign over the counter stated: 'No ladies served on their own after 10pm', which tells its own story, of course. There was no alcohol on offer, but a steaming mug of sweet tea was the perfect accompaniment to the Midnight Breakfast: steak, egg, chips and gravy, with a piled-high sideplate of bread and marge. All for half a crown.

Christmas came around quickly – a busy season for the *Evening News*. There seemed to be something happening every night of the week and I got my share of youth club committee meetings, charity parcels to distribute to the hard up and so on. Even the courts seemed busier than usual: Colly said it was the thieves' way of saving up.

One morning, a fortnight before Christmas, around the time that the pubs and clubs that ran a savings plan – five bob a week to give you a tenner for the festivities – were due to pay out their members, Colly got a phone call.

"Here we go," he said to Ted and me. "Blue Anchor club's treasurer has done a bunk with the money. I'll go and see the landlord. Maybe you can give me a hand later – get some quotes from folk who've lost their cash."

We got it into the Stop Press that afternoon, with the full story next day:

Christmas Blues for Pub Savers

Colly got the follow-up from the police within a week:

Runaway Treasurer Found Dead in Creek

Sadly there was usually a spate of deaths to cover just before Christmas, and the coroners' courts were often busy, too.

Nancy and I arranged on a Thursday evening that we'd go Christmas shopping in Pompey on next day, Friday December 4. This was my day off and we met for morning coffee at Verrecchia's, very handy for the shops in Commercial Road, now resurrected from the heavy bombing of the Blitz on Pompey. There was an ersatz copy of the great Landport Drapery Bazaar, a reborn Marks and Spencer, and Woolworth's. They were all hideous: failed attempts to rebuild what had been there before. A bus ride took us to Southsea for more upmarket department stores like Handley's and Knight & Lee, where all the women shoppers were smartly dressed with hats and gloves.

In those days, there was no question of Nancy and I spending Christmas together: her mother expected her to remain *en famille*, and my parents would have been outraged if I had asked if Nancy could join us. We decided to celebrate properly together for the New Year.

This was my first experience of a Christmas celebration 'Fourth Estate style'. On Christmas Eve there was an unexpected tingle in the air at the office. Foster joined the editorial team for coffee, just as if it was a Saturday. A messenger from head office had sent our pay across, along with the Christmas bonus. Every member of *Evening News* staff was entitled to a free turkey from the Home and Colonial grocery in Commercial Road. I'd taken my bird home a day or two earlier, to joyful acclaim from my parents – "Bless him, he's done something useful at last."

Back at the shop, I lent Foster a hand to cope with the queue of people at the counter wanting to buy the *Hampshire Telegraph*, part of its appeal being that it listed all the radio programmes for a week. In a lull we enlivened the scene by kicking the bank bag about like a football: I failed to get my head to a neat kick from Foster and the bag sailed straight through one of the little square glass panes in the front door. Cowardly, I suppose, but I suddenly discovered it was time to get the ferry to Pompey for the head office booze-up in the Bass House.

The place was crowded, the air a deep fog of blue tobacco smoke. "There y'are Ole Boy! What y'aving?" – a slightly blurred offer from Mr Gabbert, visiting from his district office at Cosham. He handed me a pint of Bass and introduced me to other reporters from outposts – Fareham, Winchester, Havant, Petersfield and Chichester – plus other young journos from the weekly papers in our area.

Now I was no stranger to strong drink, but the next thing I recall is gently being woken by Ted Brett at about 4pm, in the Reporters' Room at head office, where I had gone blissfully to sleep in Bloomy's comfortable chair, an empty wine bottle on his desk.

Apparently, Ted told me as he steered me back across the water to what he invariably used to call 'The Happy Land,' I had been the life and soul of the party at the pub and the follow-on in the office.

"Another great and noble tradition observed," he said dryly as he delivered me, reasonably recovered, to my parents' front door and made a hasty retreat.

My first year as a newspaperman ended with Nancy and me attending a New Year's Eve dance with Ted and Audrey, Mike Foster and his girlfriend and other young couples from Gosport firms at the Connaught Drill Hall, opposite the bombed-out wreck of the town hall. The organisers had put up bunting and other decorations to disguise the frankly military aspect of the place where, in my early days at the grammar school, we boys were brought for our gym classes. I pointed this out to Nancy – and complained that while the girls had had the latest vaulting horses, wallbars and climbing ropes, us poor relations had had to make-do with wornout military cast-offs. The most exercise I got there, truly, was running up the hall's cast-iron staircase, across the balcony, and down the staircase on the other side.

"That's what gave me my cast-iron constitution," I told her.

We had a couple of drinks at a table on the balcony and tried to get excited about the waltzes and quicksteps (neither of which we were any good at and frankly neither was the local band). The rest of the time we spent bravely trying to keep up a flow of chatter. It was hard-going – neither Nancy nor me was in the mood for company and I don't suppose the others were either. We left sometime around ten-thirty and jumped on a bus to Fareham.

The pubs in the main street, West Street, seemed very lively and Nancy and I soon found ourselves mixing with a bunch of other drinkers in the Market Tavern – choc-a-bloc with revellers, many in fancy dress. On the stroke of midnight everybody spilled out into the street, me in the arms of a young German girl, who kept shouting "gutes neues Jahr!" Soon everyone else was yelling "Gott Knows Yer" or some other approximation, as we all linked arms and danced our way down the street. Eventually I managed to hand my fräulein back and and to untangle Nancy from the lady's boyfriend – and we siphoned ourselves off to the park alongside Fareham creek.

We then spent one of the happiest hours of my life swearing undying love for each other....before I reluctantly took her home. Then I floated through the five-mile walk home on a rosy cloud of romance and bonhomie, shouting a friendly "Gott Knows Yer, mate" to the odd reveller I met on the way.

Chapter Ten
Suspense, Excitement, Xylophones

The New Year, 1954, began on a high note – Laurel and Hardy made another European tour and much to everyone's surprise came to the Theatre Royal in Pompey in January. They were good copy for the British papers. The story went that all through their years of their great screen comedies, the studio managed to keep their fame hidden from them. Stan and Ollie had no idea how popular they were. When their boat train pulled into the Gare du Nord in Paris, on their first-ever public appearance tour, they speculated on who the red carpet was for:

"Hey, Ollie, I wonder who the bigwig is they're all waiting for? Maybe they think we're somebody else?"

"Don't be ridiculous, Stanley. This'll be another fine mess you've gotten us into...."

They were totally overwhelmed by their reception all over Europe. They made the astounding discovery they were the world's most popular entertainers. Apparently Babe, as everyone in the business called Ollie, was only finally convinced when he found they had millions of Oriental fans in the Far East laughing and falling about at their film antics.

Pompey was no exception. There was a sketch in the live show that hadn't been done on film. On stage was a hallway, with a door at either end. Stan would open the door and look into the hallway. Seeing no-one, he'd tut-tut, look at his watch, and vanish back through the door. The second he disappeared, the other door would open, and there would be Ollie, going through exactly the same route. It was done again and again, all without a word being exchanged – a miracle of timing and expression. I don't think any other entertainers in the world could have done this. The sketch went on for an unbelievable ten minutes, the audience rolling in the aisles.

Their hilarious finale was a live version of the famous scene from their 1932 film *County Hospital* where Stan visits Ollie, the patient, who is lying in bed with one bandaged foot and leg in traction. During the course of his chaotic visit, Stan manages to inflict the maximum pain and discomfort on Ollie, all in total innocence. Another theatrical masterpiece.

And who was also on the bill at the Theatre Royal that week? *Betty Kaye's Pekingese Pets*....who could ask for more?

Our gang of young reporters at the *News* – dubbed the Bowery Boys after the American B-movie series – had a special interest in showbiz because visiting stars made good copy. And in the Fifties we still had music-hall acts in town for a week at a time. Television, of course, was about to kill that all off for ever. Some of those old-timers made an act last their whole career, but once a routine has been exposed nationally on TV, that's it.

We were regulars at the two variety theatres – the Theatre Royal and the Coliseum, later renamed the Empire. Every Friday after our 'educational' half-day release at the Muni, next-door to Charles Dickens' house (he'd trodden the boards in Portsmouth in his day), at least four or five of us would have our tea at the new Woolworth's store in Commercial Road and then catch the evening show at the Coliseum.

The barman in the Coliseum's Upper Circle Bar was Jim, once Michael Gabbert's milkman and now busy re-mustering as a mink-farming entrepreneur. So the Bowery Boys being the Press, would by-pass the box office, and make straight for the bar. There we'd pass the time sipping our halves of Bass until, given the nod by Jim, we'd step into the flies to catch the act of a favoured comic, say Terry 'Toby Jug' Cantor, or Max Wall – and whatever girlie team was appearing.

This was the heyday of the 'Artistic Tableau' as invented at the notorious Windmill Theatre in London, where nude shows were the main attraction – allowed by the Lord Chamberlain just so long as the girls kept absolutely still – and copied in theatres up and down the country. Except one night at the Coliseum, a bunch of celebrating midshipmen leaned over the edge of the box they were sitting in and dropped a few mice attached to parachutes down onto the stage. Cue screams and a panorama of moving flesh....and howls of delight from the audience.

These shows were what kept the looming death of music-hall variety at bay. They had titles like 'Secrets of the Sheikh's Harem' or, my favourite, 'Mysteries of the Orient' featuring 'Genuine Chinese Nudes.' It said so on the publicity posters.

There were acts such as The Pauline Penny Girlie Show, the 'girlies' not exactly being in the first flush of youth. And there was one time when we were entertained by a wonderful set of ladies (of a certain age) who performed a Paris-style Can-Can – while sitting down on a row of chairs. Blimey! We could hear them gasping for breath from up in the flies.

The Coliseum added even more spice to such shows by hanging a huge banner outside the theatre across Edinburgh Road with ingenious slogans such as:

Suspense, Excitement, Xylophones

A favourite comic was Terry 'Toby Jug' Cantor, whose specialty was the song *Henry the Eighth, I am*. The chorus went like this:

I'm Henery the Eighth, I am,
Henery the Eighth I am, I am!
I got married to the widow next door,
She'd been married seven times before.
Every one was an Henery
She wouldn't have a Willie or a Sam
I'm her eighth old man named Henery
Henery the Eighth, I am!

On opening Mondays, a couple of us might be sent to cover the new bill, sitting in for the regular showbiz writer Peter Jones. Otherwise we used to meet the comics and the singers in the back bar of the White Swan, the pub next door to the Theatre Royal.

Sometimes I'd get the chance to go along with Michael Gabbert to interview some of the acts after he followed Peter Jones into the job, under the byline *Showman*. I remember him interviewing a novelty act, a young lad from Holland who was eight or nine feet tall. Gabbert had himself photographed with this giant as he lit his cigarette from a gas street-lamp. The caption added: "Showman invited his guest to join him for coffee at Verrecchia's. The giant drank nine cups."

In this way legendary stories were passed around among us – of meetings with Max Miller, banned from the radio for telling this joke on air:

"Now then – I met this gorgeous bit of stuff coming toward me on the bridge. There wasn't room to pass – I didn't know whether to toss myself off or block her passage."

Frankie Howerd once gave Peter Jones a fancy pair of socks on his birthday. One night someone asked Frankie to tell us a joke.

"Forget it, " he said. "That's what I do for a living."

My fellow reporter Peter Michel and I shared an all-time favourite in Max Wall – he of the funny walks and 'My dim brother'. He'd started his showbiz career as a 15-year-old hoofer with the *Folies Bergère* in Paris, and he finished playing classic roles on TV and film. But he was out of the business in Britain for 14 years because those guardians of our morals, the whiter-than-white BBC, didn't think he was right for their image, as he'd left his family and gone off to live with a young girl dancer.

When he came back, music-hall was dead, but he was able to get theatre and film work as a serious actor, making his debut return in John Osborne's *The Entertainer* at Greenwich, and later his unforgettable turn as the creepy Flintwinch in the film of *Little Dorrit*, as well as touring university and other sophisticated theatres as a music-hall clown act, complete with his famous staircase dance.

Then there was an oddball range of hard-working comics who would do a year touring Britain on one set of jokes and routines. Peter Michel worked out that they had three main endings to a punchline: 'Now then', 'Anyway I', or simply 'Oi!'

Like this:

Stooge (begins to recite): "It's a funny old world that we live in, But it isn't the world that's queer...."
Comic: I say , I say, I say....My sister married an Irishman.
Stooge: Oh really?
Comic: No O'Riley....anyway I....
Stooge: Its a funny old world....
Comic: My wife's gone to the West Indies.
Stooge: Jamaica?
Comic: No . She went of her own accord. Oi!

Terrible. We loved every God-awful, timeworn gag, couldn't get enough. Anyway I....

Did I say that the summer of 1954 was wet? It was probably the worst summer of the whole soggy decade. Nancy and I expected to be able to spend more time together – and indeed we did. We saw an awful lot of movies. And all the time dreaming of lazy days on the beach at Hill Head, possibly a few days together in the Isle of Wight. It just never happened.

Typically, one Sunday in late June, we went by bus and ferry to Hayling Island, packing a picnic. The day started brightly, but by eleven we were sitting in a pub watching the rain drizzle down the windows. We set off back to Gosport, and still under leaden skies, stopped off at the *News* office to eat the picnic. It must have looked particularly comic to Colly as he walked in and found us sitting one each side of his desk, each eating a banana. I've never seen sympathy and mirth struggle quite so passionately on the same face. Sympathy won, of course, and he very kindly gave us a lift to Fareham in his car.

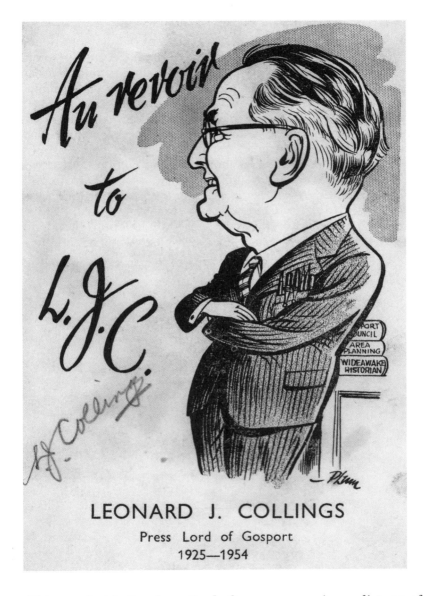

LEONARD J. COLLINGS

Press Lord of Gosport
1925—1954

This was just before he retired after 50 years a journalist, 29 of them covering Gosport, where he was regarded as something of an institution. A measure of how well the townspeople thought of him was that they elected him president of Gosport Chamber of Trade. And I loved him for giving me a crack at my dream job.

The town and the *Evening News* combined to give him a civic farewell dinner at the Tower ballroom at Lee-on-the-Solent, attended by the mayor and aldermen, the general manager of Portsmouth and Sunderland Newspapers, the editors of the *Evening News* and *Hampshire Telegraph* and all the staff. Freelance photographers came along too: the *News* only had three photographers on the payroll, so used all the local freelances including David Lawrence, whose family were an institution in Gosport, chronicling all the town's events. We were all dressed up in our 'soup and fish' (my dinner suit was one on permanent loan from Ted Brett and I wore it to every formal occasion) and, as I recall, it was what you might call a very fitting evening. The company presented him with a handsome writing desk and Ted, Mike Foster and I chipped in to buy him a presentation fountain pen. Colly had been threatening for years to write a book about his experiences when he retired. He never did get around to it.

Chapter 11
Kissing the Blarney Stone

Nancy had taken a holiday job over the summer, selling ice-creams over at Hayling Island. With my working hours, this didn't give us much chance to meet. We began to lose track of each other – one of the reasons that, towards the end of August, when Ted Brett (now in charge of the Gosport office) suggested that I take a holiday, I thought going solo would be a good idea and decided I could afford a fortnight in Ireland. I was soon to find out that Nancy had already found another god to replace me: a self-styled 'Bohemian art student' who played the trombone in a jazz band – in other words a complete wastrel.

I travelled overnight to the ferry on the 8.45pm from Euston. It was pretty crowded and I walked down most of it before discovering a compartment with four young chaps of the Army of the United States. Yanks, to me.

"Mind if I join you, gentlemen?" Politely.

"Hey, dig that accent – veddy, veddy British," said their leader, a big guy with a lot of hash on his arm; a bit younger and I might have mistaken him for a Boy Scout.

"You ain't a lord, or somethin' are you?' one of the others asked democratically.

"Ow, yers, I'm Marmaduke Bunkerton, Lord Snooty to you," I said.

Two of them moved apart to make room – and one of them clipped the top off a bottle of Budweiser and handed it to me. The two crates they had brought with them lasted all the way across England and Wales and over the Menai bridge to Anglesey and the midnight boat to Dublin. On board we found the bar open and I introduced them to Guinness.

I woke up lying on a long table, head on my suitcase, stiff all over, but feeling no pain. I stepped out on deck to see a wonderful landfall, the grinning sun rising behind us, lighting up the silvery blue of wide Dublin Bay.

In the dining saloon I had a window seat to admire the view as I tucked into an Irish breakfast of eggs, bacon, black pudding and a pint of tea. The Irish had been starving in the war: now, it seemed, was a time of plenty. Even in England, bacon had only just come off rationing.

A pair of my Yankee pals walked unsteadily into the lounge.

"Come and eat," I invited. They took one look at my greasy plate and hurried out into the fresh air. I never saw them again.

Dublin was a shock – despite its neutrality, Eire had paid a heavy price for the war. I found a land of stark contrasts: on the main streets were American cars, juke-boxes in all the cafés, and neon signs – but down sidestreets, barefoot kids begged for pennies. I took a bus ride and noted how the passengers devoutly crossed themselves every time we passed a church.

I found Phoenix Park where, in Dublin's zoo, I watched monkeys hurling themselves about the trees of their island and a colony of penguins showing off by swimming on their backs propelling themselves with their flippers with their feet pointing forward, sticking up from the water. Years later, I learned to copy them: now and again in a pool I roll over onto my back, head well back, and spin my way up and down. It's a trick I can honestly say I have never seen done by any other human. A belated thank you to the Irish penguins of Phoenix Park for the swimming lesson.

I spent the night in the clamour of the city, but next day took the steam-train to Cork. As the engine pulled out through the grey streets into green, green country I walked down the corridor looking for a comfortable compartment. And that's how I found her....she was about my age, with flowing red hair, and as she looked up I saw those fatal green eyes....a typical Irish colleen.

"Good morning," I said, "is this seat free?"

She waved a negligent hand and went on reading her book. We followed the usual ritual of strangers on a train:

"Do you know what time we get to Cork?"

"Oh, you're going to Cork, too, are you? I think we'll be there around noon...." and so on. When she spoke it was clear that, though she may have looked the part, she was no Irish colleen.

"I'm Rita Campion, from California," she said. "Come to see the old country."

By the time we pulled into Cork we were chatting like old pals. She asked where I was staying, and I said I'd look around for a bed and breakfast place.

Rita came with me to the offices of the *Cork Examiner* where I showed a reporter my Press card and asked about rooms.

"Sure, we always send people to Mrs Riley," he said. "Come away here...." and he led us to the door. "You go straight up the hill and right on top there opposite the church, there's the dear woman's digs, with the green front door. Y'can't miss it. Enjoy your stay – drop in here for a drink why don't you?"

Old Mother Riley, a shrewd-looking widow in her sixties, weighed us up on the doorstep.

"Was it one room or two you were wanting?"

As I held up one finger, Rita firmly said: "Two separate rooms, please." And the three of us went chuckling off into Mrs Riley's parlour for a cup of tea to seal the deal.

For a blissful fortnight Rita and I explored Cork city and its beautiful setting, returning each night to Mrs Riley's, only to find that she had once again mislaid her spectacles and was saying a prayer to St Anthony to find them. The first of our excursions was a trip out to Blarney Castle, Rita preferring not to look as I leaned out to kiss the famous Blarney stone, guaranteed to grant me the eternal gift of eloquence and flattery. My life depended on the none-too-sober old chap with a taste of whiskey on his breath who was holding my legs above the lethal drop.

Kissing the Blarney stone

We took the magical train ride to Cobh (formerly, under British rule called Queenstown), with its brightly painted houses lining the harbour. From this port, 2.5 million Irish had emigrated to America – and it had been the last port of call of the Titanic.

As the train ran along the wide river Lee down to the coast, a little leprechaun of a man serenaded us on his accordion with the *Rose of Tralee* and other wistful ballads. I was so carried away with it I gave him half-a-crown.

We called at Youghal, where Raleigh lived and showed off tobacco to his Irish servants, only to have a bucket of water thrown over him by a flunky who thought milord was on fire. He also brought them the potato which. as the 'pratie', became the staple Irish diet.

Youghal had recently been used as the location for the film *Moby Dick* with Gregory Peck as the redoubtable, mystical Cap'n Ahab. The waterfront was pure Cape Cod with tall, narrow houses, a general store (named Starbucks) and, overall, Hollywood's romantic reproduction of an old whaling port. The locals had cannily decided to keep the film-maker's makeover to encourage tourists to come and have a look. It worked. I found myself going down the street with a rolling gait that would have done credit to any matelot in Pompey.

In one of the side alleys an old woman stops me: "Sure have you got a spare cigarette, your honour?"

I look at her wrinkled old face, her straggling dress and shabby cloak, and give her my packet of Astoria American blend with what few ciggies are left.

She follows us around for the rest of the afternoon saying: "I'll light a candle for ye tonight, so I will. Light a candle for Your Honour," until Rita puts an arm around her shoulder and walks her with us to a tea shop.

She leaves us then – 'probably ashamed to go in,' Rita tells me.

We took a coach trip one day to the monastery at Mount Mallory, which I found utterly fascinating and truly an insight into the Catholic soul. The women on the coach, denied entry to the monastery itself, made straight for the shop to buy trinkets, while Rita – who clearly thought an exception should be made for her – complained bitterly. She had to be promised high tea at a grand hotel.

Our coach took us to the wonderful Bantry Bay and beautiful Glengarrif, to what the guide assured us was 'The Playground of Millionaires'. Bantry, drowsing in the westering sun, was every bit as your man said. The façades on the waterfront gazed at themselves in the paradise-blue waters of the lagoon, which was lazily lapping to the rhythm of soft music flowing from the hotel. Rita was, for once, dumb with the delight of it all.

"We'd get a better view from out on the water," I suggested. We hired a boat which I happily rowed out far enough so that we could feel part of the whole lyrical scene as we drifted aimlessly about on the still water. And that's how I came to hear for the first time in my life the unforgettable, heartbreaking voice of Edith Piaf, the incomparable 'Street Sparrow,' singing *La Vie en Rose*, the sound wafting serenely over the waters of Bantry Bay....

"A Day to Thank God For," the guide said in the hotel dining room, as the whole coachload of us tucked into ham and eggs and Irish barm bread (served with great balls of Irish butter), washed down with a pint of tea.

Rita and I parted the next day, she to go on to stay with relatives in Tralee – me to go back to work. It was both tearful and pragmatic; both of us avoiding any unlikely vow to keep in touch.

It was a sunny autumn day back in Dublin, but from the moment I got off the train and walked up towards the Liffey I felt a sort of chill. I went to the General Post Office for practical reasons like sending postcards and changing Irish money, but I found myself examining the bullet marks still preserved in the pillars outside from the Republicans' famous last stand in the Easter Rising of 1916. Despite the walk in the sun to the railway station, I shivered as I waited for the train to Dun Laoghaire and the ferry home, and I can still recall the strange feeling that I would never be really warm again.

Chapter Twelve
Into the Wide Blue Yonder

Being in the Gosport office was rapidly losing its charm – I wanted to get out from the grind of working the diary. I had an interview with Taffy Symons, the editor, who seemed favourable to the idea of moving me somewhere else. What I had in mind was the eastern edge of our area – Petersfield way. I'd be working the same patch which was proving so fruitful for Mary Grigg and co at *The Squeaker*. Because there were so many 'stars' living in their area, there was always some interest from the national papers. *The Squeaker's* focus on celebrities was an early form of the fever that later ran rampant in the Nineties and Noughties. If I said it had paved the way to celebrity news, that would be a wild exaggeration. But since when have I not been known for wild exaggeration?

But which new territory was I offered? Fareham. Very handy since I now had no girlfriend in the town and no particular reason to go there. I nearly turned the offer down there and then. However, I was being a bit hasty because in fact the deal was this: I would be based out of the Fareham office under the general guidance of reporter Reg Betts, given a motorbike (my old one had long ago bitten the dust), and a licence to goof off into the wide blue yonder covering the backwoods area we shared with the Southampton paper, the *Southern Daily Echo*. This was a paper sometimes so surreal that the staff re-christened it the *Southern Dali Echo*, after Salvador Dali, whom all the reporters fervently admired. The staff included Tony Brode, a poet and a contributor to *Punch*; Brian Pook, who, as crime reporter, had been known to solve murders that had baffled the police; and John Edgar Mann, who ran jazz and folk music societies. Bizarre stories were their forte.

The central village on my patch was Botley and I was supposed to cover a large slice of south-east Hampshire – Curdridge, Wickham, Hedge End, Titchfield, the Hamble river and the strawberry-growing areas around Swanwick and Warsash right down to the coast. My northern boundary was the village of Droxford with its unique magistrates court, but I would have to occasionally stand in for our-man-in-Winchester, Bob Gamble, and his villages along the beautiful Meon Valley.

Reg Betts was a sociable 30-year-old ex-RAF pilot, with a dark-haired, witty and somewhat 'fey' wife, Pauline. When we got to know each other better I'd often be invited to kip down overnight at their flat above the News office in Trinity Street. The premises were also shared by a freelance photographer, Tony Hooke, and his family. I remember Reg giving me a lesson on the brand new green BSA 250cc motorbike the *News* presented me with. I rode round and round the car park behind the office, with Reg standing in the middle shouting instructions like a circus ringmaster.

The bike may have been brand new, but it didn't take long before it broke down; we fixed it by fitting a new clutch cable. Then we had trouble with the exhaust, then the rear brake. Exasperated, I arranged for it to be collected by our garage at head office. I went down to see the mechanic myself.

"Looks like we've got a real Monday morning bike here," he said. "See that other one?" pointing to an identical green BSA in the yard. "That's the Havant office bike. The company bought them both at the same time. We've never had any trouble with Havant's bike – it's only here for its regular service."

Havant reporters Colin Dryden and Alan Biggs blissfully unaware of the theft of their motorbike. Photo: Ian Plowman

A wicked idea crossed my mind. The mechanic went off to lunch in the canteen. I went over to his bench and borrowed a screwdriver. I wheeled the Havant bike over behind a news van and swiftly removed the number plates, fore and aft. Then I took my own bike over, unscrewed the plates and swapped them round. The Devil must have been on my side because the swap went so smoothly.

I went upstairs to wash my hands and have lunch. Then I went back, nonchalantly collected 'my' bike and rode back to Fareham.

Funnily enough, it never let me down after that.

My bailiwick was a cross between the short-story landscapes of HE Bates in *The Darling Buds of May* and of John Steinbeck in *Cannery Row* and *The Pastures of Heaven*, or perhaps William Saroyan in *The Daring Young Man on the Flying Trapeze*. And the granddaddy of them all – Stephen Leacock in *Moonbeams from the Larger Lunacy* (Leacock, later to move to Canada and fame, was appropriately enough born at Swanmore, on the edge of my patch).

I revelled in escape from the tyranny of the diary; the wonderful chance to find my own stories, and generally the freedom of it all. I was supposed to phone the News Editor Mr Wilkinson at the *News* office every morning:

"Mr Wilkinson? John Bull here."

"Ah, Bull – we can dispense with the first name. You covered the Scouts' boxing at Wickham last night I presume."

"No."

"Why not?"

"I was down to meet some of the strawberry growers, so I asked the Scouts to send in a report. I didn't think it was worth more than a few pars...."

"Who do you suppose makes that sort of decision?"

"Well, actually I have to....since I'm the only one covering my area, right?"

He rang off. I never bothered to phone him again.

January and February were bitter, wintry months and riding was tricky on country lanes. But what a sense of freedom I had, swooping up and down the valleys, and conning beautiful vistas of wintry country – it was like low-level flying. I even enjoyed the night rides through the dark lanes, covering farmers' meetings or parish councils, shivering with the cold, despite Reg's thick German officer's coat from World War II and the newspapers stuffed inside my trousers to help keep the wind out. I had a cork helmet and big goggles, I looked ludicrous – but then, back in the fifties, so did everyone else.

Especially my rival newshound Miss Violet Cooke. Vi Cooke lived in Curdridge, on Kitnocks Hill, even in daylight a place dark with overshadowing oaks and pines. You would never doubt local tales that the place was haunted. Others said the high incidence of shotgun suicides in the area was because the landscape contained so many trees they starved the people of air so that depression set in....

I had been told by the editor to treat Vi Cooke carefully. She had been the *Hampshire Telegraph* correspondent for Botley,

Curdridge and Wickham for many a long year. I was supposed to cover only for the *Evening News*, leaving the parish pump, as we called it, to her. I first met her at one of the parish council meetings, where she was one of the elected councillors as well as the local scribe. She took me to one side after the meeting and told me in no uncertain manner that she was prepared to fight for her penny-a-line pieces in the *Telegraph*. I would interfere at my peril.

I thought this was very amusing and mentioned it over a pint later to Reg, who smiled a bit but didn't seem to want to talk about it.

A few days later I was on my way back from a call at the Botley vicarage, an awkward place to get to, down a cart-track covered in snow. My bike was slipping and sliding down Kitnocks Hill when I saw Vi Cooke on her green BSA Bantam. She pulled over alongside me at the verge. In her trademark black beret and long, light green mac she looked like a French Resistance fighter – an impression possibly heightened by the rifle slung across her back. As I leaned my bike against a tree, lit a cigarette and moved over to talk to her, she unslung the rifle and held it 'at the trail'.

"Don't worry, I won't be treading on your toes in the *Telegraph*, Violet," I told her. "By the way is that rifle loaded? Looks like a .22 to me."

I thought I'd made a joke. But she shouldered the rifle, worked the bolt, pointed the .22 into the air and let fly. The shot echoed round the fields and a bunch of pigeons fluttered squawking into the air.

I later discovered that Vi Cooke was a well-known competition crack shot, shooting for 'Jewels' at Bisley, the home of British marksmanship, where the prizes were – quite literally – emeralds and diamonds.

Parish councils were a staple feature of life in the country in those sometimes 'unreal' days. Wickham Parish Council was typical, a lesson in well-mannered discussion, often between people with diametrically opposed views. I learnt they'd spent long years fighting Hampshire County Council's education committee (public opinion generally agreed this lot was made up of belted earls and backwoodsmen) before they grudgingly allowed the parish school to get rid of its Victorian lavatories, sited in a leaky old shed, and to install some modern facilities.

On the agenda there was usually some talk of street lighting for a dark alley in the village. I mention this because a couple of years ago I noticed in one of the local papers that the lighting at that spot was still under discussion.

However Wickham was – and still is – proud of its heritage. I picked up a story about a chap living in one of the oldest houses in the village:

Refused to Sell his Ceiling to Visiting Yank

I'd interviewed the owner of one of the oldest, most attractive houses in the village for a piece about the growing number of tourists. He showed me the lovingly detailed plaster ceiling in the master bedroom.

"Queen Anne is supposed to have slept here when she stayed at the house," he explained, "and this tourist wanted to take it down carefully and ship it home. He offered me a lot of money, too. But naturally, I refused."

I was surprised that Americans wanted to visit Wickham – other than out of masochism – because a stone's throw from Queen Anne's bedroom stood the Chesapeake Mill, which incorporates timbers from the frigate USS Chesapeake, beaten into a bloody wreck by the British frigate HMS Shannon during the War of 1812. The battle between the two ships off Cape Ann, Chesapeake Bay, lasted less than 15 minutes but the 'butcher's bill', especially on the American side, was horrendous. Hardly surprising when the ships were yardarm-to-yardarm, blasting cannonballs non-stop into each other's guts. Shannon towed the shattered Chesapeake into Halifax, Nova Scotia, and the timbers finally wound up in Wickham.

A major story popped up in February – the Meon Valley railway line was to be closed. The *News* was determined to make a big thing of it and Reg and I, along with photographer Tony Hooke, were lined up for maximum coverage. Reg suggested that I took my motorbike further up the line and started working back towards Droxford. He'd travel on the train, we'd meet up and fit the story together.

I interviewed the stationmaster at Droxford and then went down to the pub to pick up local 'colour.' I struck lucky: an older chap nursing a pint in the corner turned out to be Jack Cook, aged 73.

"Arr," he said, "I knows all about that there railway. Should do, I 'elped build the bugger."

He and his fellow navvies had to dig out the ground – mostly heavy clay – to make a rail bed. Jack said he and his gang were expected to fill 16 wagonloads of earth a day, each wagon holding about four tons. And he gave me some colourful insights into the sort of men, mostly Irish but some Chinese too, who built the railway and lived in camps along the construction line.

I was most anxious that Jack would still be at the pub when

Tony and Reg arrived, so he could have his photograph taken, so I asked the landlord to keep Jack's glass filled up while I went off to interview other folk along the line.

We got our picture all right. Though Reg was not exactly over the moon to be asked to pay the landlord for the seven pints Jack managed to get down while waiting.

My so-called rival on the *Echo* was Dennis Stevens, another surrealist who was not only great company but also had a catalogue of useful contacts, some of which he was kind enough to introduce me to. His girlfriend ran the local telephone exchange – very handy.

He used to say: "Nobody born after World War I is worth listening to." And the stories he came up with proved he was dead right.

This was one of his typical masterpieces:

One afternoon the pilot of a light aircraft bumped down in a field near the village of Curdridge and asked a farmhand, who was baling hay, for directions – he was visiting his auntie's house for tea. He then climbed out of the cockpit, gave the farmhand a pound to keep an eye on the plane and went off to call on the lady.

After tea and cake with his auntie, and by now accompanied by Dennis, who had been tipped off by the farmhand, the pilot walked back to the plane and calmly took off, waving to his new journalist pal as he banked away.

Dennis turned in a most lyrical see-what-a world-we-live-in story. And, as always, the *Echo*, keen to encourage enterprise among its reporters, gave him a by-line 'by our special air correspondent at Botley, Dennis Stevens'.

Unfortunately he was moved to a head office job soon after I started on the Fareham beat, but he went on living in the area and I could nearly always find him in the Brewery Tap in Botley, or Roger Buckle's pub near the railway. No-one ever called it anything else – long after Mr Buckle left the place. Dennis was a friend for life: he became founder editor of *Hampshire Magazine* and later I contributed short stories for him, which he preferred to call 'commentaries'.

However, his replacement in our territory was a gift of the Gods. Roger de Houghton Beardwood moved into Nellie Spicer's guest house with his mother, a wonderful lady, classified by the locals as 'distressed gentlefolk.' They were both cultured and charming. Roger, who'd been privately educated, was a mine of classical literature and a brilliant reporter. He had 'gentleman' stamped all over him, from his well-cut suits and handmade shoes (mostly acquired I later learned, secondhand, the sort of thing a grieving widow might give to charity). He even had a slight, upper-class stammer rather like George VI. He'd lived in rural Ireland and started his career on the Irish *Skibbereen Star*, which he insisted on calling by its earlier name the *Skibbereen Eagle*, the little weekly paper which became famous for running an editorial telling the Czar of Russia to watch his step – 'the *Skibbereen Eagle* is watching you'.

More recently, Roger had been with the American news agency BUP and brought a mix of their styles with him. He was 22.

I met him for the first time in our back office at Fareham, finding him busily typing on my portable Remington:

Jerusalem, Friday

Roman occupying forces – acting apparently on the demands of local religious leaders – today carried out a formal execution by crucifixion of Jewish agitator Jesus of Nazareth, blamed for recent unrest in this volatile capital city....

I learned more about literature and, indeed, the finer points of life, from Roger than almost anyone else. And he arrived just in time for the spring re-awakening on our patch:

'Tommy, a three-year-old Exmoor pony, downed a bucketful of ale to mark the opening of the age-old Wickham Horse Fair....' we wrote for our respective papers, which freelance Jim Rudd copied for the nationals and the BBC – Jim had recently come back into my life as Fleet Street's representative for Southeast Hants and the Meon Valley (self-appointed).*

Tommy kicked off a day of funfair revelry and a free-swigging booze-up against a background of canny horse trading, with muscular young gypsy lads running through the Square exercising their ponies – dazzling, no doubt, the cohorts of girls in their best dresses, waiting impatiently for the dancing to begin – which lasted until the stars went to bed. All this had been going on since medieval times.

From then on, hardly a week went by for us hard-worked journalists without an event like this to wildly exaggerate.

In late May, the strawberry season kicked off. Our bailiwick, with some 1,000 acres of small-holdings, grew the earliest fruit in the country. Swanwick railway station sent off dozens of trainloads to

---

* The following year at the Wickham fair we used exactly the same intro on our stories in both evening papers. Why waste a good line?

London, to Scotland, and anywhere in between, with us reporters interviewing happy growers in pubs such as the Sir Joseph Paxton (who also had a strain of strawberries named after him) at Titchfield; the Elm Tree at Swanwick; and the Great Harry at Warsash. Not to leave out Roger Buckle's at Botley, where the growers' trade union, the National Farmers' Union Horticultural Branch, used to meet.

At Swanwick the scent of strawberries hung in the air for weeks after the bonanza, vying with the salty, tarry tang in the air blowing in from the River Hamble, where the yachtsmen were fitting out for the summer season.

The water regattas on the river had their own charm. This was before the days of the million-pound-yacht such as we see on the river today – correction: most of these yachts sit in the yards doing nothing, just being there as symbols of wealth. The real sailors who used to live on the Hamble, and who provided some outlandish stories for us reporters ('crabs the size of teddy-bears!'), have long sailed off o'er the horizon and into the flaming sunset.

By now Roger had found something we could show off with – a car, rotting away in a farmer's barn, left in lieu of a debt. This was a Railton Straight 8, allegedly hand-built in the Thirties for a belted earl whose crest decorated the front offside door (though it was so rusted over as to be indecipherable). Dark maroon in colour, it was an impressive, roomy limousine which attracted much attention. It seated six people comfortably in well-worn leather seats and was so steady we often used to balance a pint of beer on the floor then drive along a country lane to show off to newcomers. Never spilled a drop.

In fact the Railton was nearly 20 feet long, which was about nine inches longer than the Rolls Royce driven by the local chairman of magistrates, Col. Barrell. Roger used to take a delight in lining our Railton up alongside his in the court car-park.

Roger argued the farmer down to ninety quid for the car and then did a deal with me and Jim Rudd. We were supposed to chip in for the petrol, which cost 2s 6d a gallon. From then on we gave up any idea of competing. We went everywhere together, especially in our leisure hours when we toured the pubs with our new toy.

Roger explained: "Let's co-operate on all the regular diary stuff, and share stories from police calls – if we keep back one story a day as an exclusive, no-one can say we're not competing."

It worked wonderfully for the best part of two happy years. Though I often wondered how we managed to get away with it.

One of my exclusives, much to the annoyance of my 'partners', was the discovery that sailors at the navy training base at HMS Collingwood, near Fareham, were running a very successful pig farm as a sideline. I went along expecting to find a solitary sow in some mucky shed at the back of the base – incidentally the largest navy shore establishment in the UK. Instead I found several truly happy porkers living in pig heaven – with custom-built quarters, all spotlessly shipshape and Bristol fashion.

"What did you expect? The Royal Navy sets a high standard," Collingwood's first lieutenant haughtily told me as he showed me round.

"Headline: England expects that our pigs are the happiest pigs," I suggested.

He sighed: "If you must...."

There was a silence at this point and my reporter's sixth sense told me there was more to the tale. So I inquired how long they'd had the pigs. He decided to come clean. It wasn't just these porkers – Collingwood turned out to have one of the most flourishing farms in the district and, just like any other Hampshire farmers, they were rearing livestock and growing all kinds of crops. The farm had been in business since it was started as a wartime 'Dig for Victory' campaign in 1941. The livestock went direct to a slaughterhouse under a long-running contract, but their crops were sold on the market, save for the several tons of potatoes they supplied direct to the navy.

My story made quite a splash under the heading:

HMS Collingwood Brings Home the Bacon

Mind you, Her Majesty's Royal Navy came unstuck when they ran into the equally enterprising Jim Rudd, Roger Beardwood and me in full chase of a story. Jim was loafing about in the Victoria pub in Lee-on-the-Solent (a popular navy hangout near the Fleet Air Arm base HMS Daedalus), chatting up the barmaid.

"Lot of Wrens coming in for sandwiches and snacks last couple o'days," she said idly. "Has the navy stopped feeding 'em, or something?"

Jim's antennae went onto full alert: savvy enough to see that he couldn't start chatting up Wrens without help, he sent messages for Roger and me to join him in Lee. Even so, it took us two days of lunching in the cafés on the seafront before we found that the girls were 'on strike because of the lousy food.'

We decided to sit on the story until we had it all wrapped up – we didn't want Fleet Street descending on us in full cry. Roger charmed a couple of Wren militants into meeting us at lunchtimes over the next few days, while the story warmed up. That way we had the whole thing in the bag before anyone else got a sniff of it.

The three of us basically filed the same tale. The headline in the *Hampshire Telegraph* was:

Wrens Don't Like Soggy Dumplings

The story covered about a week of protest from the start, when some 100 Wrens out of the whole complement of 180 deserted the mess hall to eat out in Lee. One sweetheart told us: "We'd been complaining about the food for months, but nothing was done. We had some horrible brown stew the other day, I showed a soggy dumpling to the Duty Officer and asked if she'd eat it. She agreed it didn't look good, but was probably wholesome."

The base commander, Commodore Geoffrey Fardell, had ordered an investigation: the Wrens were warned not to speak to the Press and six of them were brought before the First Officer for a telling-off – all six were told they would lose their 'evening out' passes.

To which our brave informant added: "If that was done, then we all planned to walk out. They couldn't stop us. We said we wanted our own women cooks because the men just didn't understand what women wanted to eat."

Having had their say in the media, the Wrens quietened down. But months later the row blew up again when questions were asked in the House of Commons – why couldn't the navy provide women cooks? No-one seemed to have an answer.

Jim Rudd was wonderful at hooking into live, running stories. If a prisoner escaped from Wormwood Scrubs in London, Jim would file a piece saying he'd been seen in Droxford, in Hampshire's lovely

Meon Valley, and quoting a local source. Then the *Daily Mail*, or one of the other nationals, would call Jim and ask him to go and investigate. Roger and I would, in due course, be expected by our newsdesks to go and have a look, too.

The phrase 'Hampshire's lovely Meon Valley' appeared a few more times than might have been wise in stories filed by the resourceful Jim, and so he started naming places farther off, until Roger told him: "Keep the mileage down, mate, or I'll have to charge you more for the petrol."

On our free evenings, for a change, we'd try the fleshpots of Portsmouth, based on student haunts such as Verrecchia's coffee bar or the Still and West on Spice Island, the area around Portsmouth Point and the Camber. This had been the old commercial port of the city, with potato boats from Guernsey, and banana boats a regular sight: the timber boats docked further up, at Flathouse Quay.

The leader of the art-student pack was the self-styled, *'the amazing, the outrageous, the glamorous, the noisy, the beautiful Daisy.'* Daughter of a high-ranking RAF officer based locally, she spent most of her time with (equally self-styled) *'the outrageous, the amazing, the charming"* Jimmy Kelly, a colourful Irish-Canadian layabout with a piratical patch over one eye – which he claimed to have lost serving as a gunner in the Korean War. This magnetic couple shared a tiny flat in one of the warren of streets near the cathedral in Old Portsmouth.

Roger and I took the *amazing, the outrageous, etc* Daisy to a radio band-night at the Savoy Ballroom near Southsea's South Parade Pier, where we joined some 2,000 rockers and boppers to dance to Ted Heath's band. Daisy left her coat in the Railton and made a grand entrance in what appeared to be a set of feather dusters under some sort of diaphanous veil. She waited until every eye finally focussed, then turned to me:

"John darling – there's nobody here!"

As spring came on, Daisy decided we all ought to see *Jubilee Girl*, a romantic musical comedy playing a pre-West End week in Southsea. We got a couple of Press tickets and went in a group. Star of the show was Lizbeth Webb, who turned in a faultless performance as the top-drawer debutante 'coming out' in Queen Victoria's Jubilee Year, but rebelling against 'the season' and wanting to get a job in an office.

But we were also struck by the charming impact of a comparative newcomer with an unforgettable husky voice – Miss Fenella Fielding. We all agreed "Here's one to watch."

Fenella Fielding

Were we right? To leap forward to 2011.

Fenella's story is romantic in itself: she's acknowledged as a leading lady of the theatre, star of a long list of movies including the very British *Carry On* series – and darling of the intellectual critics, who often complain that she wasn't more appreciated by showbiz promoters.

Well that's as maybe – but the lady is still attracting classy notices, as she did in 2011 playing the 'wickedly malicious' Nancy Mitford in the English Chamber Theatre's *Dearest Nancy, Darling Evelyn*, based on the letters of Mitford and Waugh.

Now I thought our gang had seen *Jubilee Girl* at Pompey's Theatre Royal, but just to be sure I checked with Miss Fielding's agent. I got a phone call next day from a lady with a husky voice – you might say a thrillingly husky voice. Who else but the star herself?

"I've checked my diary," Fenella said, "and we were doing a warm-up with *Jubilee Girl* at the Kings. I played a Russian ballerina and I had three smashing numbers. I particularly remember that the Kings had old-fashioned, big dressing rooms. I didn't see much of Southsea – well with six evenings and two matinees, I'd hardly have had time. But I found a lot to admire in the old Edwardian theatre. I believe it was lavishly decorated in what I think was an Italian style, lots of gilding."

I told her that the Kings was now run by a trust, part-funded by the City of Portsmouth, and that some £2,000,000 had been spent on refurbishment in the last few years.

"They've even restored an ancient safety curtain," I said, "complete with period publicity – including the boast that "all our dressing rooms have central heating."

Fenella said: "I like that. I'd love to play the Kings again. I'm just waiting for the call."

I said I'd put in a word.

In return for us accompanying them to theatre shows, the student tribe used to goof off with us into the hinterland from time to time. There was a respectable jazz scene in south-east Hampshire; this was about ten years before the amazing rise of Country and Western music in the villages between Southampton and Pompey.

At this time a new landlord moved into the Dolphin pub at Botley, one Noel Adams. We drove there in the Railton to meet and greet the new landlord and found there was a story to it. Noel turned out to have an interesting background as entrepreneur in the music business in London and New York – and he was determined to put Botley on the map as a jazz venue. The pub was soon attracting

Dixieland jazz fans from all over the area.

One Wednesday, Daisy was in Pompey and wanted to join the rest of the arty crowd at Noel's pub for the evening, so I accompanied her on the train. She and I found an empty compartment and settled in to enjoy the ride. More and more people got on the train as it stopped at every halt along the track. Then she had the bright idea....she produced a lipstick from her pocket and proceeded to dab spots all over my face. Then she insisted on sitting me in the corner seat where I could be easily seen by anyone thinking of barging in. The scarlet-fever ploy worked like a dream....and we used it in one form or another whenever we travelled by train.

It was at the Dolphin pub one Wednesday that we met Martin Brent, a jobbing New Zealander who had sailed his 59ft ketch, Crest III, into Hamble, and later moved her up-river to Moody's yard at Swanwick. He was looking for young recruits to join him in a round-the-world trip – Daisy was the first to sign up (to plenty of nautical-type photos) swiftly followed by the piratical Jimmy and a couple of other bold spirits. The story featured in my paper, Roger's *Echo* and, via Jim the freelance, in the London evening papers and even one of the Sundays. Of course it was Daisy in her bikini that sold the story.

Martin did get the venture underway later that summer but Daisy was not one of the crew, her father having got wind of the trip and applied sanctions, such as 'no more money, girl'.

The riverside pub that was popular with the boat people was the Jolly Sailor at Bursledon, where they sold Badger beer, and it served us well too. I only knew three families who lived full-time aboard their boats on the Hamble. Nowadays the number of craft tied up there is measured in hundreds of thousands.

Another favourite watering hole was a short walk from the river, at a hamlet rejoicing in the name of Hungerford Bottom (which sounded like the setting for a Will Hay comedy), a quiet little pub called the Fox and Hounds, that time had forgotten and passed by. I used to go out there on a Saturday night with my old schoolmates, Dave and Les, mainly because the Gosport-Southampton bus passed the door. It had a handful of regulars, village folk getting on a bit, and the seating was made of cut-down barrels, but the beer was good, we could get a game of darts – and there was entertainment! A tiny old lady used to sit up on the piano stool, on a pile of cushions so she could see the music (when they used it), and her brother would accompany her on the fiddle. We went there for the sheer unbelief of it all.

I took Roger and Jim to the place. And got a shock. It turned out the landlord had decided to sell the lease – and he introduced us to the man about to take over, a cheery pilgrim called Don Taylor. We enterprising chaps told Don we would be able to give him a bit of publicity, but when we started talking to him about it, the story wrote itself. Don was a postman, fed up with pounding the round and with absolutely nil experience of selling anything at all, was going to change his life by taking over a pub.

Apart from the local publicity, between the three of us we got Don into several nationals plus a spot on a BBC radio show being interviewed by the grumpiest man in England – Gilbert Harding.

Fast-forward a bit and Don was running the Fox and Hounds so successfully he'd refurbished the old barn next door, laid out a woodland garden, and never looked back. He even marketed his own 'Old English' wines. And soon he acquired the lease of the Jolly Sailor and put his brother in as a manager. I often used to drop in with my mates and was happy to show them the story about Don that the magazine *Picture Post* ran all those years before, under Roger's byline, preserved for posterity in a glass case in the bar. Millions of yachties in their yellow wellies must have read it and marvelled.

Don was a cool customer. I was standing at the bar sipping a beer one evening when three of the yellow welly brigade were having a 'discussion' at the other end. Suddenly one of them banged his tankard down on the bar: "Don't be so bloody silly," he snapped. "I'd rather go to sea with the bloody landlord here."

Don, wiping a glass with his bar towel, didn't blink: "Thanks very much I'm sure," he said.

One day I was giving a pal a hand painting his sailing dinghy ready for the season when I noticed that the other blokes fitting out kept stopping to look up at the long pier that ran out over the mud to the deep water channel. Then I saw her.

As I remember she swayed, not walked, in a grass skirt, with a garland of flowers round her neck that emphasised the roll of her hips and the pleasurably fluid motion of her upper body. She made several trips to and from the chandler's, each time to the accompaniment of turning heads from every male in the boatyard.

I couldn't stand the suspense and headed for the chandlery to investigate – after all, it was my job. Bill, the chandler, on the promise of a lunchtime pint, told me that our hula-hula girl had arrived with a young bloke in a neat, but roomy schooner.

"The two-master tied up in the deep mid-river channel, mate," he said. "But 'tis no good you waiting 'ere till she comes back. She don't speak a word of English. Always has a list of the stuff she needs."

In the Jolly Sailor, he was good enough to point the schooner captain out, so I went over and introduced myself. This was the amazing Johnny Scott from the Scottish Islands, who'd grown up in boats and at the age of 20 had built himself a Shetland-designed yacht he could handle alone and set off for the Azores. Later, he crossed to Bermuda and then down to the Caribbean – rather like, as he said, the pre-Columbus fishermen from Scotland and Ireland, who led the way to the Americas.

"Not many people know that Columbus and his men met natives who tried to speak to them in a language they didn't understand," he told me. "It was actually a form of English they'd picked up from visiting fishermen from Britain."

The most amazing thing was that the young man had been 'given' this Caribbean girl as his crew.

"She's a real mariner herself," he said. "Indeed she built the schooner. She copied the hull from a wreck washed up on her island long before. And she directed me and some of the local boys doing the actual work. But it was her design, based on the shape of the craft, and made from locally grown trees. Those islands are famous for the shipbuilding qualities of their timber."

What a story. All I had to do was persuade the girl to pose with Johnny Scott for pictures – which she flatly refused to do. I kept hoping.

One day I rolled up to the riverside and the schooner wasn't there. My chandlery pal handed over a note....saying how sorry they were but the customs and immigration men were taking an interest in them and they'd decided to move quietly on.

"Pint of Badger, please, Don," I ordered, "I've got sorrows to drown."

The summer, with its seasonal country shows and languorous days on the beach, wore smoothly on. The Fareham *News* office became a meeting place for us journos and sundry 'sources', so many that Reg threatened to put up a sign – The Palace Flophouse – borrowed from our favourite book, Steinbeck's *Cannery Row*. This was partly motivated by my inclination to take a short siesta after (or instead of) lunch, a quirk which later developed into a lifetime habit. I used to doss down on the piles of newspapers stored in a back room awaiting collection by a head office van which never came.

I recall a strange story that the others didn't get a sniff of. A friendly copper tipped Reg off about a robbery near the riverside village of Sarisbury Green – "there's an angle to it that I'll leave you to find," Reg said, cryptically.

The scene of the crime was a small 'news, conf, tob' dubbed 'The Shed', a green hut nestling under the trees at the roadside. I walked in through the open door, and into a bizarre tale:

A tall, vigorous looking chap in a neat suit stands behind the counter.

"Hello, stranger, what can I get you?"

"Are you Bill Botting?"

"Yes."

"I believe you were robbed yesterday. I'm from the Evening News and I'd like to write a piece about it."

"Are you really a reporter?"

"Yes. Here's my Press card."

"Don't bother with that, I can't see it – I'm blind, you know."

Enter a young girl.

"Mornin' Angela. Usual?"

"Please." She places a ten shilling note on the counter.

Bill reaches behind him, takes down a packet of ten Gold Flake cigarettes. Picks up the ten bob note and drops it into a drawer, from which he takes some change and puts on the counter.

"All right, Angela?"

"Yes, thanks, Bill. See you later."

"Not if I see you first."

And I find myself laughing with them at this little joke.

Bill tells me he hasn't been robbed. Someone got hold of the wrong end of the stick. Then he gives me the real story.

" I've been blind since I was 18," he said. "As well as running The Shed I play the piano accordion and run a dance band – we do quite well locally. I've always said I can tell my customers from the way they walk across the floor, not just by the voice. And I've only got it wrong once in 27 years.

"This bloke came in and, thinking I recognised him, I said 'Hello, Sid.' No reply. I thought it might be the new postman, so I walked round and touched his coat. Then he hit me. Didn't hurt much – but I was pretty upset and started wrestling with him and yelling for help. People ran in and separated us – and it turned out he was deaf and dumb. Of course, he had no idea I couldn't see him."

I wrote a feature story about him for the *News*. And whenever I passed that way I used to drop in on Bill for my fags.

"Hello, here comes the Press," he used to say.

As we covered the summertime flower and produce shows from Warsash to Wickham, Roger grabbed the opportunity to entertain a series of girls picked from the stallholders and carnival entrants.

But one young lady, in whom he took a keen interest, we met at Fareham Magistrates Court. She was accused of careless driving, which in those days was treated rather more seriously than it is today. The case for the prosecution was being conducted by a police sergeant, a real country bobby with a red face and drawling accent to match. He took his witnesses through their stories well enough, then sat down.

The Clerk then told the smartly dressed blonde in the dock that it was her turn to tell her side of the story.

"Thank you," she said, then turning to the sergeant she said: "Is that the end of your case, Sergeant?"

He gave a little smirk towards the bench as he nodded. "Ah, yes. That'll be the end of my case, then...." He didn't actually add 'Missy', but you could hear it in his voice.

"I submit that there has been no evidence to show that I was the driver of the vehicle concerned," she said briskly. "Therefore I would ask Their Worships to declare the case closed."

The copper's jaw dropped. The Press sat up straight. The clerk turned to whisper to Their Worships on the bench. Col. Barrell in the chair finally announced that the case be dismissed.

Roger and I nearly fell over each other in our haste to follow the stranger as she picked up her bag and headed out the door.

'Blondie' turned out to be a barrister on the south-western circuit. Nice one. Last I saw of her, she and Roger were heading off to a smart teashop in the High Street. Jim and I phoned the story all round.

Once a month a court was held in Droxford, next to the police station, covering cases from the Meon Valley. We used to like going there because it was never arduous – and was opposite the White Horse, whose landlord Phil Marshall, an ex-naval officer, had instituted a bar known as the 'quarterdeck', haunt of Meon Valley 'characters' well worth cultivating by journalists.

We hardly ever got a story from the court, but one of the best was a case we couldn't report on the grounds of taste. It concerned a farmhand accused of bestiality with a pig. No newspaper would touch that sort of thing, of course, but we listened in anyway, Roger, Jim and me, and a bloke from the *Hampshire Chronicle* at Winchester. The four of us crowded round a small card table marked 'Press.'

The farmhand went into the dock, looking terribly shamefaced, as well he might. I like to think he was defended by our old pal Archie Kingswell, but memory may be a bit faulty here. Anyway, the defending advocate questions the chief witness, a village lady who lives opposite the piggery:

"I must thank you, Madam, for allowing me to see the view from your bedroom window."

The lady nods.

"And you say you saw the offence being committed from that window?"

"Thass quite right, zur."

"But between your window and the pigsty I must say I noticed there's an advertising hoarding which hides your view. Yes? So how could you see what went on?"

"Ar, zur, I saw un undoing his trousers as he went be'ind the board....and then I saw un come out later from the other end, doin' 'is trousers up – an' he had a smile on 'is face."

Of course, the magistrates have no choice but to dismiss the case. On his way out, our victorious defending solicitor pauses at the Press table, leans over to me and whispers:

"I should have asked if there was a smile on the face of the pig."

Just as the Wickham Horse Fair in May marked the end of dark days and kicked off the outdoor fun of carnivals and shows in our Hampshire villages, the season's closer – traditionally on the last Monday in October – was the celebrated Titchfield Bonfire Carnival, also said to have its roots in medieval revels.

Titchfield Abbey came into its heyday under the Normans, when it became a popular venue for royal weddings. Naturally it was sacked by Henry VIII along with other church enterprises up and down the country in the Dissolution of the Monasteries and handed over to one of his supporters, Henry Wriothesley, first Baron of Titchfield.

His son became a patron of Shakespeare's (and at one time was fancifully identified by a leading academic as the 'dark lady of the sonnets'). In earlier days Titchfield had been a river port. Imports came up the River Meon from the Solent and the English Channel, it then being navigable by small coastal craft. However, Wriothesley's son, the second Baron, is said to have blocked off the river for some scheme of his own, thus putting local businesses out of work and bringing hard times to the village.

So they burned the wicked baron in effigy and whole village turned out to spit on him, so to speak. The tradition has been kept up ever since, with additions from Guy Fawkes.

In my day the event, lovingly organised by the Titchfield Bonfire Boys, attracted some 5,000 visitors and brought in a handsome sum for local charities. It consisted of

Titchfield Abbey

two processions through the village, afternoon and evening, in fancy dress, or as tableaux on the back of a lorry, and a huge bonfire, with effigy, of course, and spectacular fireworks in the evening. There was always a visiting funfair as well.

Reg and I arrived early enough for lunch and, by invitation of the landlord of The Bugle, the old coaching inn, we were given the first-floor front room, overlooking the Square, centrepoint of the celebrations. The landlord offered us a drink, but we politely settled for coffee, knowing full well how much ale would likely be going down this day.

We gave in about an hour later when Roger and Jim arrived. By now the colourful floats were arranged all over the Square and surrounding lanes. They were mostly mounted on lorries, but with quite a few on traditional carts pulled by horses and one tastefully arranged with many bouquets of flowers carrying Miss Titchfield and her Princesses (chosen a week earlier at a Saturday dance).

Miss Titchfield was crowned with due ceremony, the crown being placed on her head by last year's carnival queen. Roger, with his sharp eye for girls remarked: "Hey, she looks exactly like the new one!"

Reg, who'd been covering the event for a few years, explained that they were sisters. "There's four younger ones in this family – enough to carry on until 1960, people say. This is a highly competitive thing, you know, taken very seriously indeed. Many family feuds started with a row over the choosing of the carnival queen. Indeed some old-timers would tell you that Shakespeare pinched the idea for the family bust-up in *Romeo and Juliet* on one of these feuds."

Jim was looking rather thoughtful at this point, so I ordered up another round of drinks to take his mind off flogging the idea to Fleet Street. Might well have started another feud.

The judging over and the afternoon procession well under way through the cheering crowds that lined every street and lane in the village, Reg suggested that we say in our reports that the crowd exceeded 5,000.

"Whoa back," said John Prentice, our Fareham office manager. "Head office will want to know why I haven't sold thousands of papers if there's that many here." So we settled on 3,000 as a compromise. John had set up his Bush machine at the Bugle to stamp the racing results into the Stop Press column on the back of a huge stack of newspapers. This machine, which printed from a stencil, was the size of a desk and just as heavy, but was still described as 'portable'.

He and Reg were still arguing about numbers, so Jim and I decided to take in the funfair. Apart from the rides, the shooting gallery and the Dodgems, where the voice of Kay Starr over the panatrope was breaking everyone's heart with *Wheel of Fortune*, there were the freakshow booths to investigate.

There was, of course, a bearded lady, a very ordinary-looking woman who could have been anybody's mum – except for the bushy, straggling shank of hair hanging down from her chin to her knees. Then there was the monkey with two heads; the world's strongest man ripping telephone books apart barehanded and waving impossibly heavy-looking dumbbells; the flea circus, another tradition; and – best of all – Miss Pringle's Performing Pekes. Jim wanted to take one home with him....until I reminded him he already had some playful kids of his own.

I recall wondering why I bothered to be a sensation-seeking reporter when there was all this on view for sixpence a time.

Chapter Thirteen
A Strange Creature in the Kitchen

K nocking around with a mixed bag of students in what Daisy always referred to as 'Our Golden Age' meant I never lacked for female company. I was alone, however, on a rare warm and sunny afternoon when I rode my motorbike down to Hill Head for a dip in the sea.

As I was drifting off to sleep in a post-swimming mood, I heard female voices prattling away in French. A few yards away, two young girls were stretched out on one of the sandy stretches between the shingle, in their rather primly old-fashioned swimsuits – what ever happened to the Brigitte Bardot look?

"*Bonjour mesdemoiselles,*" I called out, and we were soon chatting in a mix of cross-Channel babble – me endeavouring to speak French and they trying out their English. We got on surprisingly well.

It turned out they were both au pairs working for families in Titchfield and this was their afternoon off. It was also the start of a rather nice friendship for me and the slightly older of the two, 19-year-old student Annie Rivière. As they left to get the bus back to Titchfield, the other girl, Monique, came back and slyly handed me a slip of paper with a phone number – "Annie say I give you telephone of the family, if you like call her." Then, blushing and giggling, she ran off over the shingle to the (rapidly) retreating Annie.

Annie was a true Parisienne, daughter of a lawyer, very well-educated in the French manner, and a mine of information on French movies and existentialist writers. She and I met as often as our respective jobs allowed and there was also a rare bonus in it for me: apart, that is, for charming company with a warm-bloodied real life girl to kiss and cuddle, it turned out she was a minor goldmine.

We used to talk about the French films I'd seen – we were both great Jacques Tati fans – and we would re-run bits of the movies together, especially the bit in *Monsieur Hulot's Holiday* where the English wife keeps handing her husband tiny stones, or shells, which he throws away the moment her back is turned. It was a pleasure we never tired of, wandering up and down the beach, me trailing slightly behind, carrying out this pantomime.

Like most of my contemporaries at that time, I was fond of a bet now and then on the horses: my grandfather had been a bookies' runner. I mentioned this one day to Annie – and to my surprise she said, matter-of-factly:

"There's a horse going today which you should bet on. It's being ridden by a friend of my father, French jockey Serge Boulanger, who is spending the summer riding in England."

The horse, Tudor Jinx, obliged as they say. I said *"Phew!"* as I sank to my knees in relieved gratitude. I'd put my whole week's pay – £5 – on the nose, God Bless Jinx and Serge for romping home at 5-1.

So Sunday found Annie and me off to Pompey and onto the steamer to the Isle of Wight. I made a mental note that girls generally like a touch of sea air, especially the bit where we had to huddle together when the steamer turns into the wind. We were equally pleased to have a compartment to ourselves on the impossibly quaint little green steam train – a period piece even then. In those days the line ran through from Ryde Pier to Sandown and Shanklin, then on to Ventnor – through the Victorian tunnel dug under the downs. Annie and I certainly had a day to remember. She was entranced with Ventnor, a seaside village neat as a jewel, clinging to the slope of the downs and full of Victorian gingerbread cottages and villas.

"Oh, John," she said, *"mais c'est plus que magnifique.* It is just like a little French seaside town. It's exactly like the place in *Monsieur Hulot's Holiday."*

And you know what? Whenever I chance to go there, I can still see it like that, through her eyes – though I have to squint a bit to take away some of the twenty-first-century additions which are more 'tatty' than Tati.

We strolled about and came to a little corner dress shop.

"Une très-boutique boutique," she called it.

I found a dress – dark blue with white polka dots – and suggested she try it on. The shop assistant diplomatically complimented me on my taste, of course. But when Annie came out of the cubicle, even I believed I had some some talent that way. In that blue dress she was as French as *salade Niçoise.*

And after a neat little lunch at a typically genteel teashop, we ambled slowly uphill, past the fork in the road, with one sign pointing *'To the station'*, and the other *'To the station, easy way'.* As the witty Yogi Berra once said: *"When you come to a fork in the road – take it."*

At the top of Ventnor Down, we dropped onto the grass, exhausted by the climb. We lay there dozing in the sunshine, Annie waking now and again to peer admiringly into her shopping bag, to reassure herself that her new blue dress wasn't a dream.

We had come out at the top of the high down above the tunnel, the brick-lined open end immediately beneath us. We could hear the rumble of the approaching train. Annie sat upright with her legs stretched out wide apart and, as the little green engine rushed out of the tunnel in a cloud of steam, she hollered:

"Oi, John, *regarde*....I'm giving birth to a train!"

Minutes later she was plucking up grass, sniffing it and saying things like: "You know, John. There can be nothing more wonderful than to die in beauty...."

I'd never met anyone like her, didn't know such people existed. She introduced me to a young (she was 18) French writer, Françoise Sagan, who was picking up a following outside France for her novel *Bonjour Tristesse*, and who was noted for her romantic themes, her disillusioned characters and a ludicrously extravagant lifestyle. Her adherents later insisted that *Bonjour Tristesse* (Hello Sadness) influenced Paul Simon's pivotal *The Sound of Silence*. I wouldn't be surprised.

We travelled back on the charming little train, and spent the ferry-crossing standing at the taffrail watching the curling white wake stretch back to the island, 'rolling up the past' she said.

A week or so later I called for her at the home of the navy couple she worked for in Titchfield and we took bus to Hungerford Bottom to the Fox and Hounds to show off her new dress to Roger and Jim and some of our art-student friends. I think Annie and I were carried away under the romantic spell of the garden on a summer eve (and Don Taylor's Old English wines). We fell asleep and were woken by Don clearing up just before midnight. By a miracle, we made the last bus to Gosport and – having phoned her host family to explain – I took her home to sleep in my bed (....no, no, I dossed down in the spare room).

I was woken by my mother in the morning: "There's a strange creature in the kitchen, using my gas stove. She says she's making your breakfast."

She was too. Blue dress and all. Great girl Annie.

Neither of us had any illusion about keeping in touch. She had exams to go back to. I had a date, too. My country apparently needed me....

Chapter Fourteen
Two Years Out of the Ink

One morning back in the spring I had received an ominous OHMS letter inviting me for a free medical at the Royal Hospital, Portsmouth – a nice offer, except it went on to reveal this was a preliminary to my call-up for two years' National Service. All blokes had to do this at 18, or as soon as their apprenticeship or college course ended.

Two years out of the ink – I might as well give up all hope of getting to Fleet Street. But I had a plan, like a lot of other enterprising guys. We even had a reporter on the *News* who 'engineered' a septic toe and had it amputated so that he'd be found medically unfit. He kept the toe in a jar of spirits on his mantlepiece and used to show it off to people at parties. Ironically, he later changed his mind and volunteered to sign up for a short service commission in the Army and spent best part of three years in Jamaica.

Actually my plan was somewhat simpler. Rather than submit to soldiering on £1 10s a week, I would go abroad until I was 26 – the age for exemption – which was quite a popular alternative among better-educated young men. My plan was to go to Dublin, get a newspaper job and use that as a stepping-stone to moving on to New York.

Ian Reeves and Nettie Kelly at Howth harbour

I organised a holiday in Dublin with my school pal Ian Reeves, who was what we'd call today 'a petrol head', and off we went. As I thought, he took to Dublin and particularly to all the American automobiles in the city and quickly discovered he could hire a car far cheaper than at home. We put up at the Horseshoes Hotel, Parnell Square, then a lively part of town with a noisy dance-hall just down the street from our room. There we met another holidaymaker, Nettie Kelly, by coincidence the same name as a cousin of mine.

In the morning, we all drove down in Ian's hired Chrysler to Howth harbour to see the fishing boats, and

I remember buying a parcel of fresh herrings, for sixpence, which we took to our hotel for them to serve for our high tea. And then we went off to Bray Head, where the Wicklow mountains join the sea.

Nettie and Ian got on well, so next day I was able to slip off to the Press Club to see about a job. I chatted to a reporter on the newly launched *Dublin Evening Herald* who suggested I call his Chief Reporter. I did it there and then. The chief, Mr CF Linane, suggested I call into the office at about 4pm.

After the introductions, he said: "What do you say we go and discuss this over a pint?" And he led me to a watering hole nearby. Clearly he expected me to convince him I was worth the hire – and he encouraged me to talk about the stories I'd covered. After a couple of pints, he looked at his watch, sighed, and put on his hat.

"All right, fella," he said "I'll take a chance on you: how does seven guineas a week sound?"

I was gobsmacked. It was two guineas more than I earned at the *News* and in Dublin you could live at a small hotel for ten shillings a week, all found. Seven guineas was Rich! I nearly took his hand off when we shook on the deal. I was to start as soon as I could work out my month's notice with the *News*. Meanwhile I could pop into the *Herald* in the afternoons for a while to get the feel of the action.

The blow fell three or four days later.

CF took me to one side. "Come and have a drink," he said. I knew from his manner it was bad news.

"I'm sorry, son," he said, pushing a Guinness and a whiskey chaser my way. "You and I haven't been keeping up. Behind our backs the British government, and ours, have done a shabby deal to close this National Service loophole. It's recent, but it is cast iron, the company lawyer says."

"So I can't join you?"

"It's just not possible," he sighed. "You're gonna have to be a soldier. Maybe you'll come and work for me after you've done your bit. So keep your head down."

I never went back, of course. And many years later, on holiday with my wife in Tuscany, we were met by a young Irish courier and guide named Linane.

"Any relation to CF?" I asked.

He grinned at me: "If you mean the highly respected, and widely honoured editor of the *Dublin Evening Herald*," he said, "I must admit to being his son."

And then, of course, it was drinks all round.

It was drinks all round, too, at my departure for the RAF early in mid-July. Reg and Pauline Betts had recently moved from the *News* flat into their dream house on the northern edge of town overlooking open farmland rolling away to the horizon and, as far as I know, all the way to Birmingham. And they were kind enough to open the house to the vast numbers of journos and newspaper staff, art students, photographers, solicitors, police and firemen, nurses and other medics glad to come and drink my health – as long as it meant seeing the back of me.

The events of that farewell party passed so far into local legend that Michael Gabbert, down from his new job in London for the weekend, always maintained they'd never met anyone who would admit they were not there. Gabbert, never noted for exaggeration (he claimed), even went so far as to say he'd never met an art college girl who didn't boast she had 'given her all' as a fitting send-off to John Bull.

I'd say that was physically impossible – but then how would I remember?

It was all very abrupt: one day I was a freebooting reporter, the next I was just a number. However, I did make one crafty move on the way to National Service. Armed with a travel warrant to RAF Cardington in Bedfordshire, I stopped off in London and headed to Fleet Street, where I had a school friend who also worked for the *News* – but in the London office. None other than the lovely Brenda (the Jean Simmons lookalike) I'd admired for all these years. We enjoyed a good lunch, swapped life stories, and got along very well. I left, a bit wistful, but vowing I'd get in touch when I was demobbed.

Chapter Fifteen
Despatches from the Front

RAF Cardington, Bedfordshire: *Joining-up routine, July 1956. My civilian clothes are taken away and I parcel them up to send home, making a complete pig's ear of it. I'm fitted out with a uniform, very like the uniforms I'd worn as a cadet. I'm now officially Aircraftman Bull.*

A telegram arrives from the editor of the Portsmouth Evening News*: 'Do you intend to return to News on demob?' I telephone, saying that it is indeed my intention to return in July 1958. To my surprise, the editor tells me my pay will be made up, including all rises and bonus payments as they come due. Who could refuse?*

I proudly show the RAF my certificate of passing the Aircrew Selection tests at RAF Hornchurch back in 1952, but they say I am only eligible for aircrew training as a pilot or navigator if I sign on for three years. I immediately start to look for loopholes.

RAF Hednesford, near Cannock: *I complete eight weeks' of basic training at this boot-camp (drilling, shooting and fieldcraft) on pay of £1 10s week. I elect to train as a wireless operator, otherwise known as a WOP – this should allow me to become aircrew and thus get around the three-year rule.*

RAF Compton Bassett, Wiltshire: *In six months at No 3 Radio School, I struggle to learn morse messaging but finally make 25 words per minute. Meanwhile I audition for the RAF radio station along with Aircraftman Alaistair Sutcliffe, who is also a journalist. We become Record Presenters (the term 'DJ' has not yet been invented). a couple of days a week, spinning discs like* Take The 'A' Train, *and* Green Door.

While awaiting a posting, I'm put on Pool Flight, which means they dish out chores for me to do. I am asked to build a road from the Officers' Quarters to the Officers' Mess some quarter of a mile away. I study books in the library to see how to go about it. I start with digging out the track and laying large stones, then – thanks to funds from the Officer's Mess – I'm able to hire the groundworkers from a local builder's to do the fill-in and to cover it all with tarmac. The whole job is finished inside two weeks and I invite the Chaplain to cut a ribbon to declare the road open. Some 40 years on, I get a call from Alistair Sutcliffe to tell me that the MoD are selling off Compton Bassett and wondering if I'd like to pick up a souvenir or two at the auction. Sadly, I'm unable to go, but Alistair reports back that my road is still in good nick and is now owned by a farmer who bought the land.

RAF Upavon, Wiltshire: *I'm pleased to be sent to the headquarters of RAF Transport Command, visualising myself flying around in huge great aeroplanes, but new radio technology means that morse is no longer needed – and nor are Wireless Operators. Instead, the signals officer appoints me as his secretary and I find I'm in charge of issuing documents, including 48-hour passes. I become very popular with the men in my billet.*

The signals sergeant discovers I am a touch-typist and wangles me a trial as a Teleprinter Operator (TPO), which I pass with flying colours. I'm promoted to Leading Aircraftman (LAC) – and

receive a propellor emblem to sew on the sleeve of my uniform. On my watch, I find Corporal Edna – the fastest typist I've ever seen – and I watch in disbelief as she copies a signal, at the same time as reading Woman's Weekly. *There were no errors in the signal, and she has clearly absorbed the magazine article as well.*

I come to the attention of the boss, Air Marshal Sir Andrew McKee, Air Officer Commanding Transport Command, RAF Upavon (affectionately dubbed 'Square'). He uses me as his 'fingers' to 'talk' over teleprinter links with his subordinates all over the globe – except, as he says, when radio links are interrupted by African witch-doctors talking with their drums. (I think he made that up). I am promoted to Senior Aircraftman (SAC) and get a new propellor badge with three blades.

Air Marshal Sir Andrew 'Square' McKee

On watch in Libya: has somebody pinched the plane?

Exercise Rosie-Rosie: *I am 'invited' to join Exercise Rosie-Rosie, which means attachment to Akrotiri, the RAF bomber base in Cyprus, during the terrorist emergency in which different factions are struggling for control of the island. Fully kitted out in denim khaki uniforms, our group flies out in a giant Beverley transport aircraft nicknamed the Elephant of the Skies. I am put in charge of group of signallers living in a rather pleasant bungalow, overlooking the Mediterranean. We do a lot of swimming. On one occasion, we are attacked on the beach by terrorists who open up with a Bren gun. We all take cover and no-one gets hit. Back at camp we are addressed by a veteran flight sergeant: "Well boys, now that you have been under fire, you will probably be eligible for a medal." My oppo, Alfie, nudges me: "Will you tell him or shall I?" – "You tell him."*

Alfie says: "Look at us, flight sergeant – see, we're all war babies. We were being bombed in our cradles. In fact we're quite used to it, sir." (Collapse of stout party, as they used to say in Punch).

We move up to a temporary camp near Nicosia. Bored with hanging about, I acquire some secondhand clothes from a Cypriot driver and nip off into town in my free time. But one afternoon I am rumbled by a British colonial policeman, an Irishman, who gives me a stern lecture on staying out of trouble and then takes me to the skating rink "where Madame serves the best and coolest brandy sours on the island." He then gives me a lift back to camp.

Royal Naval Hospital, Haslar, Gosport: *On leave on a 48-hour pass, I collapse and wake up in Haslar Hospital, less than a mile away from home. This gives me a couple of wonderful, idle weeks recovering from an appendix operation: they serve me a Guinness every lunchtime and 20 cigarettes every day. My mother visits and – knowing the ropes from visiting my father here during the war – is savvy about what to do with the duty-free ciggies I slip her.*

Once mended, I report to the Captain of Haslar, as every leaving patient has to do.

"Ah, Able Seaman Bull," he says, the rank the navy kindly gave me when I arrived. "I've had a very strange signal about you from some RAF chaps. They want me to send you to HMS Daedalus at Lee-on-the-Solent, so they can send an aircraft from RAF Upavon to take you back."

"That's great, sir," says I.

"I can't possibly be a party to sending Other Ranks flying about the country," the stiff-necked bugger tells me. As a result, I have to spend the best part of a day travelling back to Upavon by bus and train – only to be sent straight back home again for a fortnight's recuperation leave.

RAF Upavon: *I'm back in the signal section, this time as a shift leader. The winter is vicious – a tramp sheltering in a shepherd's hut on the downs is found frozen to death. We have to clear snow off the runway, with a tot of rum to keep us going.*

Fireman Bull: *In the spring, I am one of the thousands of national servicemen selected to train as a fireman. After demob and in the event of nuclear war, we would be liable to be called up to join Civil Defence Flying Columns. This means a wonderful month at Blackpool – 'noted for fresh air and fun' – followed by another month at fire service headquarters at Moreton-in-Marsh, Gloucestershire, where they give me a Matchless 500 motorbike to ride shotgun for our Flying Column as we tour a series of lakes and clay-pits, flinging more water at imaginary fires.*

A great end to a distinguished RAF career.

Chapter Sixteen
Five-to-One on Blue Boy

As the train passed over the River Hamble at Swanwick, I leant out and spun my RAF cap clear of the bridge and watched it fall into the tideway. Done with that.

Back home in Gosport over a cup of tea Dad handed me a letter from the NUJ – an invitation to attend a weekend union training session at Southampton University. It just happened to be that weekend. We had a debate about it – Mum wanted me to stay home while Dad, definitely a union sympathiser, won the debate. As he said, it would be an excellent way of getting back into the job.

"Hang on," I said, "Gabbert and some of the boys are bound to go to this. We've always been quick to take advantage of a free weeknd on the NUJ."

So instead of taking a train to Southampton, I got the bus to Fareham. Trusting to luck, or gambling on my mates' sense of nostalgia, I stood outside the *News* office in West Street, leaning indolently against the building and casually smoking a cigarette. It was a longish wait, and there were three butts on the deck when, just after six, Michael Gabbert pulled his Standard Vanguard up outside the office.

Someone opened the rear nearside door and I calmly slid into the seat uttering that timeworn cliché: "As I was saying before I was so rudely interrupted...."

Gabbert was accompanied by three new faces: Micky Knipe, Colin Webb and Trevor Fishlock, none of whom, of course, showed the least surprise. Peter Michel had decided to go on his motorbike. Naturally the weekend turned out to be my 'welcome back' party. What we hadn't reckoned on was that we were no longer junior reporters – no more the Bowery Boys, but older, responsible adults.

We had been replaced by a new thrusting bunch of newcomers determined to behave every bit as notoriously as their legendary elders (us) had. When the local pub shut at ten, this crazed mob, armed with bottles of stout, marched round and round the campus singing their little hearts out and keeping everyone up till the small hours. The best we ancients could do by way of landmark was to cart Peter Michel's motorbike into college – where astonished staff and students hurrying into the refectory for breakfast found it in pride of place on the top table. The new cub reporters got the blame, but as Fishlock explained to them, they had learned a lesson that would sustain them throughout their new careers – "There's no substitute for experience."

The Uni got their own back by banning the NUJ from the campus for ever.

I assumed that I would take over where I left off. During my two weeks' demob leave I went down to the Hamble and consulted boatbuilder Alan Moody – I figured a houseboat on the river would suit me fine.

"I've got just the thing for you. It's an old riverboat from India – you know, British Raj and all that. Belonged to an old India-hand, Army wallah who retired back here and had the old vessel brought over."

He called a rigger over to show me around the vessel, lying on the mud handily placed opposite the Jolly Sailor alongside a couple of hulks needing tender loving care. She was about the same length and width as a wartime MTB, the main section aft being the passenger cabin with a once-elegant mahogany door. The old captain's key fitted and the lock turned but we couldn't budge the door for the empty bottles, mostly gin, jamming the way.

"The skipper drank himself to death," the rigger commented laconically. "Hard to say which was the more derelict, him or the boat."

Clearly there was an awful lot of work to do to get her shipshape, but as the rigger pointed out she was a sturdy, roomy craft, ideal for a chap on his own. We settled on a price of £150 for the vessel and £1 a week rent for the berth, electricity and water. I suspect the power of the Press had something to do with the terms.

The *News* were expecting me back at the end of July, but when I called to confirm my restart, I found myself talking to my old antagonist Wilkinson, who lost no time in giving me a good kicking.

"We'll be needing you in Head Office," he said, "mostly covering the courts. So I'll see you at 9 o'clock sharp on Monday. Good day."

I watched the return to my *Pastures of Heaven* and my riverboat disappear with a puff of a fag.

Well, of course, I had to move on, no use looking back. Indeed this had been made clear to me earlier. Towards the end of my RAF days, home on leave, I invited my old love Nancy out. We enjoyed a pleasant enough evening and wandered a little dreamily about our old haunts, more or less for old times' sake.

Then as we parted, she said something very important to me.

"You know, John, looking back I'm glad we never went all the way....I like to remember us the way we were – romantic, first love, and all that."

A chaste kiss and a dream no-one could ever take away.

In my first week back I was teamed with a new reporter, Phil Griffiths, recruited from Petersfield. We covered the magistrates court, the county court, and the Quarter Sessions – all still housed in temporary postwar buildings, and all close to the Queen's Hotel in Southsea. Outside the sessions court you could still see where sandbags had lined the entrance in World War II.

Over a lunchtime pint in the Queen's, Phil said: "Be handy if we lived here in the hotel – wouldn't have far to walk."

"Be perfect," I said, "but the mean old sod (meaning Wilkie) would be sure to find some footling reason not to let us. I doubt if it would cost more than thirty quid a week all in."

Since our pay was about £10 a week each, Phil thought this was probably true. We were still laughing about the idea as we strolled along Osborne Road towards the Crown Court for the afternoon session of civil cases. Phil stopped suddenly and poked me in the ribs and pointed to a tallish villa on the corner virtually opposite the hotel. In the front downstairs window was a discreet 'Flat to Let' sign.

The rent was two guineas a week, including electricity. It was possibly the most ideally situated residence I ever had. The Hall Floor Flat, as Mrs M called it, had a tall front room overlooking Kimbell's ballroom, the Figaro – our favourite Italian cafe – and a cakeshop on the corner. Lipton's grocery was a few yards away.

Kimbell's was the ballroom of choice for local organisations such as the Chamber of Trade, Rotary, Inner Wheel, and the local big firms. It wasn't long before Phil and I were volunteering to do other reporters' night-jobs at Kimbells (always two tickets), so that hardly a week passed when we didn't get a free meal just for scribbling a few lines from the after-dinner speeches.

In the flat we had a roomy bedroom with two single beds, a quaint, spacious bathroom, and a neat little kitchen. The big front lounge was dominated by a huge sofa with a back so wide people could lie full length on it. There was a fireplace too, and that autumn the Hall Floor Flat became the preferred rendezvous for *News* reporters and their girl/boyfriends on Sunday afternoons. Peter Michel was a dab hand with a couple of loaves and a toasting fork in front of the fire. Also on offer was an array of delicious cake from the corner shop, cut-price because they were yesterday's.

Pompey had about a dozen cinemas then – and the *News* carried crits of three or four major ones on Tuesdays, we reporters covering the films on Monday evenings as allocated in the diary. But frequently we were able to divide the films up over tea on Sunday so that we went to the films we wanted to see, wrote them up and swapped the crits around on Monday when we found who was down to cover what. It worked well because of the wide variance in taste among us – and it meant that often we had Monday night off.

After a while, Phil and I became more involved with the stage shows. There were three commercial theatres – The Kings, The Theatre Royal and The Empire (formerly the Coliseum). In earlier days Peter Jones and Michael Gabbert had covered the music halls, but now that they were both working in London on showbiz papers. Phil and I shared the showbiz coverage between us.

There was also the summer season at the little theatre on South Parade Pier. I was there to cover the matinée one afternoon when Tommy Trinder was the lead act. Now Tommy was often billed as the 'Prince of the Ad Libbers' and this time he got that bit bang to rights. Imagine a routine in which Tommy is interrupted by a stooge bringing him a telegram.

Tommy opens the telegram, reads the message and mugs shock and surprise to the audience. Trouble is, the stooge hasn't gone off – he's just standing there.
Tommy says: "You waiting for a tip?"
Stooge nods.
Tommy: "Blue Boy in the three'o'clock!"
Exit Stooge.

Exit me too, having checked my watch to see that there was just time to phone a piece in for the Late Extra edition:

(Note to subs: ONLY USE IF BLUE BOY WINS 3-O'CLOCK AT SANDOWN) **Sharp-eared members of the audience at South Parade Pier this afternoon were on a winner when Tommy Trinder ad-libbed a line on stage – 'Waiting for a tip? – Blue Boy in the three o'clock!'**

Blue Boy did us proud – at a very nice 5 to 1.

And I am pleased to say that is just the way it happened.

Phil's girlfriend Pat was a professional dancer, which helped his bona fides as a showbiz reporter. I treasure the memory of applauding a musical at The Empire which featured Pat and the girls in a number called '*A-huntin' we will go*', with the chorus-line in obligatory tight, short jackets and miniature skirts to show off their legs.

'Tantivy, tantivy, tantivy, a-huntin' we will go' – to cheers from the stalls, mostly filled with happy-go-lucky matelots.

The Theatre Royal of the old music-hall days had died on October 20 1956, while I was serving my country in the RAF. The last two shows featured good old Max Miller and Vic Oliver, a fitting farewell both to the 100-year-old variety theatre and to two guys deeply associated with the old music hall. However, the *Hampshire Telegraph* theatre writer, Charlie Green, when asked to write an obituary for music hall, came up with something better – an interview with a young actress appearing in rep at Worthing, who suggested that the lovely old theatre's future lay in repertory: not amateur stuff but the real McCoy, proper plays put on by a proper company of actors (not unlike Charles Dickens' rep company in *Nicholas Nickleby*). A couple of years later, when I returned from serving my country, that's what I found.

The Theatre Royal rep company was led by Hector Ross and his leading lady was June Sylvaine. They were pretty good and had a lively following, but running the theatre – especially one that included a drama school with four young players – was just not profitable. By September the Royal was set to close, but was rescued by Portsmouth's theatre 'angel' Commander Reggie Cooper (who with his wife Joan also later saved the Kings Theatre), enabling Hector and June to carry on with their repertory company.

Theatre manager Geoffrey Wren was well aware of the value of publicity and Phil and I often were invited to his house in Old Portsmouth, handily round the corner from the Still and West, to be charmingly entertained by him and his lovely French wife. Geoffrey also fitted up a small bar in the basement of the theatre, where the Press and our friends were encouraged to drop in and meet the actors. We reporters leaned over backwards to find titbits of news about the Royal to keep the place firmly in the public eye. We ran stories about youngsters getting their first showbiz break; we ran stories about old-timers dropping in to lend a hand; and we shamelessly filled the gossip columns (what we called 'Diary' stories) with the most trivial items – an actor taking a holiday and returning with a tan was among the most ludicrous.

We even featured June's new cat, Suma. She had wandered into the theatre one day to shelter from a rainstorm – and never left. Phil dreamed up a story that Suma was to have a 'walk-on' part in a production of John van Druten's play *Bell Book and Candle*. But it was not to be: on the opening night the cat went down with a tummy bug and missed her big chance.

Among my casual girlfriends at this time was a dark-haired, dark-eyed beauty known as Bea, the new waitress at our favourite Italian café, Figaro. I offered to take her out on a Sunday afternoon and I made a big impression when I showed up just as her church was calling time, in a horse-drawn carriage (arranged by a mate). Bea was completely bowled over by this and chattered excitedly as Dobbin ambled around the streets of Old Pompey before dropping us off for the ferry to Ryde. I recall she bought a couple of tiny glass animals which she set up on the mantlepiece at the Hall Floor Flat. Bea was never very forthcoming about her home life, which remained a bit of a mystery.

But after all, she was at the Figaro most nights and I often used to have my dinner there with or without Phil, the owner of the café, Freddie, having decided to treat us as 'family' along with a special cheap price on the Spag Bol. I walked in unexpectedly one night and sat at a table. Bea appeared from the kitchen, saw me, and dropped the tray she was carrying – with three plates of cannelloni, two coffees and sundry soft drinks. The mess on the floor was impressive.

I tried to help – until Freddie arrived, took one look and ordered me and Bea out of his sight. Pronto. Amazingly he didn't fire her. But I did, when I met her by accident in the street one day. She was with some of her pals, all in their neat school uniforms. It turned out Bea was only 15.

At this point Phil went down with some bug or other which called for him to have his tonsils out – it is easy to forget how primitive medicine was in the 1950s. For instance, whatever happened to Ulcers? In the 50s, 60s or even the 70s it was the great scourge of the overworked businessman. Hardly a Hollywood movie was made without a caricature of a boss worth millions who was not allowed ordinary food – he had to down a pint of milk every half hour *BECAUSE OF HIS ULCERS*!

Somewhere along the way this dreadful scourge slid quietly off the radar. What happened? Did we suddenly find a cure that wiped out ulcers? Was it like the Salk vaccine that did for the horror of polio? Answers on a postcard, please.

Back to poor Phil, home from hospital and feeling mighty sorry for himself. I found myself making him little treats such as jelly and cream, minced fruit and custard, until I got bored with being a nursemaid. I took to spending my evenings with the *News* gang at the nearby Apsley House pub, playing darts. Until one night Phil showed up looking remarkably fit and well, apparently able to sink pints of Bass.

Suddenly the door of the bar was flung open and a spitfire hurtled in – Bea, howling blood and guts. She launched herself in my direction and aimed the contents of a saucepan straight at me. Somehow I leapt out of range and the whole stew exploded over the floor. Bea fled into the night and Phil took off after her, leaving me to clear up the whole squeaking, bubbling mess to the great glee of the journos and Vic the landlord.

Apparently Phil, in his miserable, weakened state had been unable to resist Bea's offer to make supper for both of us – the idiot just forgot to mention it to me.

Our idyllic autumn in Pompey came to a climax with the inevitable closing down of the old Coliseum. The sale of the place, to a supermarket chain, was the final act we'd all been dreading. No more girlie shows, no more Chinese nudes, no more 'middies' letting mice run around the stage, no more old-time comics – relics of the old music halls. The end.

They put on a special show and an auction of memorabilia on the night the curtain came down for the last time. A whole gang from the *News* was in at the death. Peter Michel did us proud with a very moving piece about an elderly retired music-hall star who happened to be visiting Pompey and found the old Coliseum was about to go down. Heartbroken, he came to the party. Peter's story appeared the next day:

Out of the Night Came an Old Trouper....

I got a telephone call at the office to ask me to come to the theatre and collect my memento (apparently, under the influence of maudlin nostalgia, I had bid a shilling for a large stag's head, complete with antlers, that was used as a hanger in the stars' dressing room). Phil and I set him up in the Hall Floor Flat and christened him Stanley. From there he was handed down from scribe to scribe, as reporters came and went. Years later I met him in a harbourfront flat occupied by three girl reporters at the former home of Colonel Wyllie, the marine artist.

Chapter Seventeen
Our Man in Battersea

Throughout that autumn of 1958, Phil and I had been waiting for the call to come from Gabbert to say he'd found us jobs in London. As well as working for a showbiz weekly, he was moonlighting with shifts at *The People*, the Sunday rival to the *News of the World*.

Almost simultaneously he found a vacancy on the *Romford Recorder* for Phil, and an interview for me at the *South London Press,* a high-circulation bi-weekly which came out on Tuesdays and Fridays. I got the job, packed my bag and headed for big-city life.

The *SLP* covered all ten boroughs in South London from two offices, at Streatham and Elephant and Castle. It was owned by two brothers, known as Mr John and Mr Frank. One reporter covered each borough: mine was Battersea, with 100,000 souls. We were not encouraged to hang about the offices, but to get out into our 'manor' and dig for stories. We could return in the afternoon to write up our copy and use the phones. It was tough for me at first because I'd been working the courts and theatres at Pompey and was out of the habit of digging out stories.

That December was bitter cold. Picture this Dickensian scene: young man, 23, not much spare flesh, tramping the foggy, damp or freezing streets off Clapham Common and Lavender Hill....in a thin mac and fashionable (but leaky) winkle-picker shoes....

God knows how I survived. I spent an inordinate amount of time in the Express Dairy café, or Battersea Town Hall foyer. I phoned my mother to send my old ex-navy submarine sweater, a thick, huggy-buggy jumper made for Arctic seas, and my duffel coat with the fake-fur collar. Out of my first 15-guineas-a-week payday (I'd lied about my age in order to get the 'seniors' rate given to 24-year-olds), I bought some fleecy-lined boots.

The day generally started with police calls, carried out as a team with reporters from other papers covering the borough, to save us all wasting the Old Bill's time by calling individually. So we met in the Express Dairy at 10am: Ross Werge, of the *South-Western Star*, one of a chain of small, more parochial London weeklies; Dave Pote of the *Clapham Observer*, also one of a chain; and me. Ross was regarded as the senior man on grounds of having been there longer. Occasionally we were joined by some beardless youth from the *South London Advertiser*, a newish publication trying to break into the boroughs, that found it hard to keep staff due to the low wages they paid.

We all trooped along to the police station on Lavender Hill, next door to a popular Metropolitan Police watering hole called The Cornet of Horse, always referred to ironically by members of the 'Met' and the Press as 'The Cornet of Horse Of Course' – because none of us could ever recall why it was named after an ancient army rank, and a very junior one at that. Still it was a nice pub. We tended to work together on any stories we picked up from the police, such as street accidents, fires, or kids getting their heads stuck in saucepans. Similarly, we pooled resources when we were invited to attend hospital committee meetings and all kinds of routine photo calls. Outside of that, it was the usual story: all out for a scoop.

I may have been out of practice, but I realised that unless I developed a thick skin to call on people, I'd simply perish from exposure. So I started dropping in through any door I found open. On the *News* if you wrote a story featuring a businessman, it would be spiked on the grounds of 'giving him a free ad – let him advertise with us, for cash.' But the *SLP*, as I soon discovered, had no such inhibitions.

Desperate one bitter morning when even the struggling Battersea Tory office (the borough was virtually 100 percent Labour) had nothing to tell me, I ventured into the ironmonger's down the block. He had a small oil-fire going, so I started chatting. It turned out he was about to instal a novel 'make your own paint' machine called the 'Rainbow'. The customers chose from a selection of different hues – and the machine mixed up the paint and put it into a tin. I wrote a short piece about this back at Streatham office and handed it over to 'Max' Wall the news editor, expecting him to hook it straight onto the spike.

"Hey, this is good," he said, beckoning me back to his desk, "Can you organise a picture? It'll make a decent page top for Tuesday. This is good for us – 'Rainbow Over Lavender Hill – Bright Idea Brings New Business."

A few days later he handed me a list:

Industry in Battersea

Price's – candle company
Manbre and Gartons – sugar
Morgan Crucible – metal-casting crucibles
Projectile Engineering – metalwork
Battersea Power Station – electricity generation.

"There you go," he said, "here's a useful source of stories for you: we've been neglecting this area. See what you can dig up in the way of the Romance of Industry."

"Why not?" I thought. "At least I can keep warm in these factories; the power station is bound to have some kind of furnace." Not half – as I was soon to discover. I went on a tour of all the big factories and wrote up lyrical descriptions – of rows and rows of different coloured candles, for instance, the pride and joy of Price's world-beating products.

When I got to the power station, I was fitted out with an asbestos suit and the thickest set of anti-glare goggles ever made, just so I could see inside the great furnace. You could have driven a horse and carriage through the entrance, so vast was the opening of this 'fireplace', the world's largest furnace. It was being fed with coal and coke by an army of sweating, blackened-skinned stokers.

My two guides told me to put my goggles on, then they opened the hatch for my glimpse of Hell. And that was exactly what I saw. Hell, hell, hell – a great searing sunburst of blinding heat. I stepped back, gasping for breath as they slammed the hatch shut and stood grinning at me.

"I never, ever, want to see anything like that, ever again," I said, and they nodded and took me off for a pint of (cold) tea.

My first month or so I spent in a miserable guest house in a Clapham back street. A quick look at the 'Hints to Guests' and you knew right away that the boss, Mrs Allsop, had been a seaside landlady. The main meal was at the ludicrous hour of 6.30pm sharp. The cottage pie, or corned beef hash and cabbage, was always augmented by a large plate of bread and marge. If I was not there sharp at 6.30pm I found the most long-standing resident, a taciturn young Irishman, Enda, had scoffed the lot. The only bright spot in this mean set-up was fellow guest Henry Wong.

Henry was a true generous spirit as well as a subtle comedian. If I wasn't working in the evening I'd knock on Henry's door and we'd settle down to listen to foreign jazz stations on his super shortwave transistor radio (Sony, of course) which, though not much bigger than a fag packet, seemed to be able to cover the globe. The superior American Forces Network (AFN) was the favourite of favourites for the jazz records alone.

Everything Henry did, or owned, he belittled out of Chinese politeness.

"That's a nice pen you have there, Henry."

"No, no, you have very much better pen. Very superior to humble instrument here."

The exception was the Sony, of which he was unashamedly proud.

He satisfied my reporter's curiosity, explaining that his 'honorable father' (he called him 'Dad') had sent him to England to study and work in a bank....and to become more English than the English. His sister was sent to study at a business school in New York, to become a perfect western housewife and mother to a whole tribe of Yanks, and his older brother went to work and study in the capital of Communist China, Peking as it was called then. Papa Wong was hedging his bets for the future.

One evening I found Henry carefully gift-wrapping a truly exotic silk dress – one of those with a revealing slash along the thigh, a *cheongsam*.

"Present for pretty girl at LSE," he explained. "I ordered it from a pal in Hong Kong. Hope I got the right size."

I admired the colour and feel of the superfine silk.

"I say," said Henry, "why don't we get one for you? I'm sure you have girl in mind, perhaps? Price very reasonable...."

And that's how Rose, my old buddy from the arty crowd, came to be a sensation in her peacock-blue *cheongsam* one night back in Pompey in the Still and West.

This may have reminded me that I needed a girlfriend of my own. So I kept my pre-National Service promise to Brenda and called her up at the *News* in Fleet Street – phone in one hand, fingers crossed on the other.

"Hi, Brenda, it's John Bull. I've just got a job on the *South London Press* and I wondered if we could have a drink, say this weekend?"

"Wonderful to hear from you, John. Glad you've got a London job, but I can't make it this Saturday, dear – because I'm getting married that day."

The groom was a chemical engineer – and they had a very happy marriage. I went back, miserably, to my lonely room.

I was finally rescued from my digs by another reporter at the *SLP*, our man in Lewisham, Dave Trenbirth, known to 'Max' Wall as Mr T. He shared a tiny flat with a travel agent and pub-piano player, fellow Brummie Ron Bowater. But, he told me, they had found more roomy quarters and needed a third person to share the cost of four guineas a week.

So I found myself living in a flat on Clapham Northside, where Trenbirth and I often cooked an evening meal together in our little kitchen (the 'Joe' – cockney slang for a piano player – being fed at the pub). Two nights a week we dined out – Thursday, which was payday, and Monday, when we collected our expenses. We had two main eateries, The Shakespeare's Head at Victoria for a cold beef

JB and Mr T in a typical pose

salad and a pint of old ale, and the life-saving George's, a Northside spaghetti joint where we were allowed credit if broke. We also used to drink with George's Italian waiters in the local pub.

In those days life in South London was dominated by back-bedroom revolutionary politics, small groups with plans to take over the world – by argument or preferably by blowing things up. The Boot League (extreme right wing), the People's Crusade (extreme left), and outfits like the Tolpuddle Vengeance (Up the Workers), met in rooms above shops and offices throughout the *SLP's* ten boroughs. Typical was a meeting I attended with Trenbirth above a pub, opposite Clapham Common tube station.

Dim lighting, a smell-of damp clothes (it was a dirty night on the streets and rain was dripping through the roof into the room). A sprinkling of young men with beards and earnest specs, a middle-aged woman or two – probably teachers – prematurely greying and carrying net bags bulging with paperbacks. Someone at the back starts speaking....

"Brother Wilkins, I wish to draw the committee's attention to a letter in Friday's *SLP* in which Comrade Meacher, under the guise of contributing to the current campaign for a change of voting rules, is clearly making an early campaign speech – which as you know is against rule 14A of the league's constitution....(shouts of disagreement)."

Very depressing. I whispered to Mr T : "How did that get past Max and into the paper?"

He whispered back: "Ah, but Mr Kenton, our editor, loves all this sort of stuff. He's a member of five or six of these looney groups – and he does the letters page himself."

Mr T was a tremendous help to me as he had been Our Man in

Battersea before being upgraded, and he handed over his list of contacts. As Battersea was nearer than his territory in Lewisham we often cruised over over there, sometimes on my newly acquired Francis Barnett motorbike, or more often in Mr T's 1938 Morris 8. When the weather improved in the spring. we spent more of our time back over the river in Chelsea at such popular pubs as the Six Bells, or the Man in the Moon.*

As a rule, *SLP* reporters didn't cover courts, which were handled for the paper by an agency. But now and again I would drop in at Battersea court, if only to enjoy a chat with Ross or Dave Pote, my rivals. On one such day, Ross and I had decided there was nothing doing and packed it in. I was a bit slower to leave and I had my hand on the doorknob when I heard the magic words from the witness box spoken by a young girl applying for a pub licence:

"I am applying for the licence for myself," she told the court. "My parents, who are also in the public house trade, bought the White Swan at Battersea for me as a twenty-first birthday present...."

What girl gets a pub for a coming-of-age present? I promptly returned to the Press table. As soon as the girl had got her licence I approached her and her parents outside, showed my Press card, and asked if I could have a chat. Her name was Mara Starling and her folks kept the well-known Dog and Truck at Stepney. I was on the phone to Michael Gabbert within the hour. The upshot was that when Mara opened up as the landlady of the White Swan, he and I were there by invitation, along with Lawrie Manifold, news editor of *The People*, and the paper's photographer, Stan Janus.

It turned out the White Swan had been a regular venue for London's famous blind bandleader George Shearing – think *September in the Rain* and the evergreen *Lullaby of Birdland*.

Needless to say we all had a great evening; *The People* ran the story bigtime on Sunday, and I got a right royal roasting from Max on Monday for scooping my own paper. I mollified him a bit by supplying a longer story with lots of local South London interest and some extra pictures for our Tuesday paper, complete with 'Best wishes' from George Shearing in America. Max and the editor Mr Kenton (known as Mr K) were both newspapermen first, and 'angry boss' second – so they ran the story very big indeed.

* Dave Trenbirth had succeeded to Lewisham after Brian McConnell left the *SLP* for Fleet Street. When Rupert Murdoch's Soaraway *Sun* was launched, Mac became the news editor. Later, when a loony gunman tried to shoot Princess Margaret in Pall Mall, Mac – who happened to be passing – leapt in front of the princess and took the bullet. He was later given a hero's medal.

Meanwhile, I took my chance to ask Lawrie Manifold for a regular Saturday job at *The People* (worth a handsome seven guineas per shift).

"I tell you what," he said, "you find me three more stories like that and the job's yours."

Over the next two months I did – and needless to say, he didn't.

Trenbirth and I got into the habit of popping up to Birmingham to see his Mum, Glad, and his Dad, Sid. We were there at Easter for the opening of a brand new saloon bar at Birmingham racecourse, Trenbirth hitting the jackpot with a rank outsider called Panche Calyon. Since then, in our circles, anyone who has a blindingly lucky inspiration is said to have had 'a Panche Calyon moment'.

We alternated weekends in the Midlands with trips down to Pompey, sometimes staying with my Mum and Dad, but more often crashing out with some of the newspaper/arty crowd.

And then there was Robina, a red-haired Glynis Johns lookalike with huge green eyes, once seen never forgotten. I'd met my match with this one when, as a young airman, I'd been released 'mended' from RN Hospital, Haslar in October 1957 and had taken the ferry to Pompey to celebrate. I'd walked into the favoured upstairs bar at the Still and West and found this heartstopper sitting Goddess-like in a black velvet dress and a string of pearls emphasising a complexion best described as flawless.

Robina

"If you were mine those pearls would be real," I'd told her. She had rewarded me with a cynical twist of the mouth, a long pause while she weighed me up, and then the warmest smile anyone ever gave me. She had been delightfully easy to talk to, witty, clearly well-read, and had played the 'cynical loner' with easy charm. We'd spent the rest of the evening chatting before she had to return to the nurses' home at St Mary's Hospital where she was training.

I never forgot her. A week or so later I'd sent her a postcard from London, but got no reply. I'd phoned the nurses' home a couple of times and we had chatted, but she never kept the date we'd made (I only discovered later that she'd been ill with pneumonia.) We'd started meeting early in the New Year, though I only had 'visiting rights' to call for tea at the caravan she shared with another nurse, parked on spare land behind Fratton Park, home of Pompey football club.

Meanwhile, back at Ranchero *SLP*, things were warming up. It was a time when I kept getting into tricky situations. I felt a vague feeling of trouble ahead....and I wasn't wrong.

It started with a phone call from Michael Gabbert one Monday afternoon.

"Meet me at 5.30 outside Swiss Cottage tube station," he said, "we're going to pull off a stunt. Look out for me on the main road, I'll be in Nellie" (his Standard Vanguard).

Sure enough, a little after half-past he came cruising up to the kerb and I opened the door and jumped in.

"See the story in yesterday's *People*?" he asked.

"The Yankee sailor with his 15-year-old bride? I'm surprised there wasn't more, given all the fuss about under-age sex. Where were all the banner-wavers and...."

"Right," he interrupted. "The US Navy has put a block on publicity, but I managed to get a look at the address of the people they're staying with....and that's just where we're going."

We turned into a side street and I spotted the house straight away – the whole of Fleet Street seemed to be camped in the tiny front garden of a terraced cottage halfway down the road.

Gabbert parks up and we stroll casually towards the house. We both adopt a 'we live here' attitude and march through the crowd and up to the front door where Gabbert bends down and calls through the letterbox: "Hello Auntie," he hollers, "here's John come to see you."

A burly-looking bloke opens the door a crack and Michael, with a merry "Put the kettle on", walks straight in with me in tow. As I close the door behind me I hear one of the mob outside say, "Here, that's Mike Gabbert isn't it?"

In no time Michael and I are sitting down with the young sailor and his child bride, let's call them Frankie and Belinda Jane, drinking tea and chatting away like old friends. It turns out that the burly chap and his wife, 'Auntie' to us – at least for the day

— are a couple of real Cockneys and distant cousins of the sailor. Their problem is how to get rid of the Fleet Street mob outside, who keep slipping offers of cash in return for photos and a story, through the letterbox. Meanwhile the American Embassy officials are trying to straighten out the legal points of importing an underage bride into the United Kingdom.

As usual, Gabbert has worked out a ploy.

"Look," he tells young Frankie, "we know how to get rid of the gang outside. It's quite simple: if you agree to sell your story to one paper only, to the highest bidder that is, you'll find the others will just walk away."

"But tell me, Buddy, what will they do to us if we agree?"

My turn: "Well, if it was me I would take you out on a tour of the sights of London. Take a photographer with us — take romantic shots of you at, say, Buckingham Palace, the Tower of London, Westminster Abbey, Trafalgar Square, Piccadilly Circus, and the Embassy of the good, ole U S of A."

Frankie can see that Belinda Jane is loving this bit. But, what about his captain and the US Navy?

Michael takes over. "OK if I call your embassy and put the idea to them?"

Frankie's still a bit doubtful, but Auntie comes to the rescue, bringing over the hall phone as near as the lead will allow, and handing the telephone directory to Michael.

"Hello, is that the United States Embassy? Can you put me through to your Naval Attache?" A pause.

"Hello, sir, my name is Michael Gabbert and I'm speaking on behalf of your sailor with the young bride....yes, the one with newsmen crawling all over him."

I've never admired Michael more than the way he handled that tough American sailor/diplomat. The upshot was that we telephoned the *Daily Express* newsdesk, offered to sell the story as an exclusive, and made arrangements to bring the couple in to the paper.

Then came the tough bit and a typical Fleet Street nasty car chase as Michael and the *Express* reporter took the scenic route to the office, with me and their snapper right behind them in his tiny sports car, trying to hold up the pursuing heavy mob. We were doing a detour around some quiet lane off the North Circular when a big car from a rival bunch, expertly driven, went round us and forced us into a ditch. The car picked up a few dents and scratches.

I'd escaped with a few bruises – the photographer was equally lucky – and we were able to drive back to the *Express* office, known to all newsfolk as 'the black Lubyanka', after the notorious Moscow KGB prison.

Michael and I shared £50, less his car expenses; the happy couple pocketed £100. And they had a delightful tour of London next day. The ship sailed slightly earlier than scheduled, so there was no further fuss about Belinda Jane.

Around this time a prisoner doing five years for robbery with violence escaped from Wandsworth jail. The hue and cry made the nationals, since this villain was said to be dangerous – and there were appeals for him to give himself up. One of the evening papers carried a grainy picture of his wife with a kid in a pram, stating that the girl lived in Battersea. I noticed that the pic had been taken in the busy Battersea Bridge Road.

Of course, I clipped it out and on a busy Wednesday morning, I took up my position outside the Latchmere pub. I'd been there an hour and a half, smoked five fags, downed two halves of beer and was about to call it a day when:

There she is. Pushing the pushchair with kid straight towards me.

"Hello Sarah," says I, and while she is still bewildered, I gently lead her away.

"I'm neither a cop nor a grass," I tell her. "I'm with the SLP. We're on your side, love, and I want to give Joey a break."

She says nothing. Doesn't know what to do.

"I don't want to know where Joe is," I reassure her. "I just want to talk to him. Here's my name and number – it might help him if I can give his side of the story."

Back at the office that afternoon Max handed me a piece of paper with an address on it. And the words 'Thursday 10.30.'

I showed Max my cutting. "You plan to go there?" he asked. "It's up to you, but he is said to be violent."

"I checked. He has no previous."

"Well, do you want someone to watch your back?"

"No. His pals will be watching," I said.

"Good luck, Mr B – don't get hurt."

I didn't. Joe was a nice guy. He convinced me he'd been framed and an easy target for the Old Bill to get a quick conviction. We ran his story – and he got a retrial and an acquittal. And I was a proper reporter at last, with genuine form.

My next scoop, I think was more important on the scale of things. Battersea Dogs Home was, of course, on my manor and I used to phone regularly for information. They usually wanted me to run a picture of some hard-luck case pup who needed a home. Max, the editor Mr K, and the brothers wouldn't hear of it. For a change one day, I decided to drop in instead of phoning. The Superintendent, an ex-Army captain, greeted me cordially enough and offered to show me round. I found myself shaking paws with spaniels, dachshunds, labs, cavaliers – some in single kennels and others, presumed more companionable, in spacious compounds.

"I thought I heard a cat, just then," I said to my guide. "You did," he said.

"Oh sure, I suppose you keep them here, too?" I said wittily.

"Come and see," he said, leading me off to another part of the home. The miaowing got louder as we approached. Sure enough there were dozens of the little furry creatures washing, eating, purring, snarling (when I put my hand on the wire) or blissfully asleep.

"How how many of them have you got here?" I stuttered, gobsmacked.

"About 30 at the moment," the captain announced with pride. "We may be famous as a dogs' home, but we've been looking after cats for 50 years."

A scoop, or what? Battersea Dogs' Home was known all over the English-speaking world. A delighted Max headlined it:

Secret Shame of Battersea's Dogs

As the summer of 1959 came on (the only sunny summer in the whole decade), union unrest in Fleet Street and across the newspaper industry began to warm up. There was an election coming and printers' trade unions, fed up with Harold MacMillan as prime minister, were trying to stop newspaper owners from filling their papers with Tory propaganda. The clamour of the political intelligentsia in the *SLP, Clapham Observer, South Western Star* and *South London Advertiser* was growing into a crescendo and dominating the news pages.

Unrest boiled over into a strike in Fleet Street involving the inkies, the print unions, and the Newspaper Proprietors Association. However, the provincial press (including local weeklies like ours) were not involved – until some unions decided to widen it out.

As far as the SLP went, some of the print unions, including the National Graphical Association (NGA), downed tools and also some of the production unions, members of NATSOPA. Union and management agreements meant our lean team of NGA blokes came out, but the owners and the apprentices could work on – so with Mr John and Mr Frank rolling their sleeves up, we were able to print a slim, if amateurish, version with a limited number of papers. The strike went on for weeks becoming increasingly bitter in Fleet Street and at the SLP there were always a few flying pickets dropping in, mostly the NATSOPA heavy mob.

Trenbirth and I and a few others, including Max and the editor Mr K, used to meet in the evenings in the pub we used for our regular union meetings. Trenbirth and I left early one night to walk back to the office and pick up his car. The street outside Leigham Court Road was being patrolled by some NATSOPA heavies, under the eyes of our own NGA boys. Suddenly a rumpus broke out around the side door where Mr K was trying to get into the building. I saw a NATSOPA thug strong-arm him away from the door. Trenbirth and I didn't hesitate: we bashed straight in. All we were trying to do was jostle them away from our boss, but it turned nasty.

I remember Trenbirth and one of our printers, their backs to the wall, punching anyone who stepped forward. I charged from behind and leapt on the back of a burly figure who went straight down to the ground. Then I was in the thick of it, trying to keep a guard up and punching well below the belt. By now, reinforcements had arrived, so that we had the thugs between two fires, so to speak. I realised the bloke helping me was Dave Pote, the hefty South African reporter from the *Clapham Observer*. With more than a little help from such friends, we finally saw off the attack – at the cost of bloody noses all round. Pote had a lovely black eye. We retired to a pub to recover – and it wasn't until the next day I realised I had broken my left index finger. It never did properly straighten out.

Pote wrote the story up for the *Clapham Observer*:

Bloody Battle at the SLP

Thanks, Dave. Stirred up by the publicity, the mob came back on Thursday night and attacked the vans which were waiting to distribute the limited number of papers we were able to print. They tipped sugar into the petrol tanks, totally immobilising the fleet. There was worse to come: Mr Frank was helping out in the machine room as the papers rolled off the press. Suddenly there was a 'web break' in the long run of newsprint roaring through the machine and the paper swept through the air at speed – just like a scythe. Mr Frank saw it coming, put his hand up protectively and the flying paper sliced off a couple of his fingers.

The brothers were even more determined to get the papers out: they came up with the idea of an 'emergency edition' of the *SLP* – a 'leaflet raid'. Their plan was to use a helicopter from the new experimental heli-pad on the Thames at Battersea. Max, of course, sent for me since I had contact with the people running the heli-pad.

"Just explain the idea," he said. "If they are interested, we'll see how many papers we can get to them."

Aah, the best laid plans: someone who couldn't resist it tipped off the BBC and the unions threatened action against the heliport.

The bosses then decided I should take my two weeks' annual holiday to get me out of the way. The country was enjoying the rare heatwave of 1959 and I wasn't unhappy about the idea. My wonderful Robina had qualified as a nurse and left St Mary's Hospital, so we had a couple of blissful weeks of sea and sun. We used to ride over to Hayling Island on my motorbike, find a remote spot among the sand dunes, and pretend we were all alone on a desert island.

On our last Sunday evening, Robina arranged for her flatmate to do the nightshift at the private nursing home where they both worked. She cooked me a simple Italian meal, we finished off the Chianti and fell asleep lying on cushions on the floor, with our feet stuck out on the balcony to cool down. (By now I had overnight sleeping rights – provided I behaved myself). We were rudely woken by thunder, lightning and torrential rain, 'Wagnerian style', our feet and legs soaking wet.

I proposed as I was rubbing her down and she accepted me.... with a typical Robina get-out clause: on condition nothing was said to anyone until much later.

Chapter Eighteen
The Only Weekly that Comes out Every Day

Something had changed in me. Trenbirth was the first spot it, sometime in late September, as we cooked a couple of chops in our tiny kitchen.

"You'll be leaving soon, I expect," he said.

"Whatever gave you that idea?"

"Your heart's not in it any more buddy, everyone can see that."

Dave was a real mate (and still is, even though he lives at least 3,000 miles away in Halifax, Nova Scotia, and we meet only once every decade).

I confessed that Robina and I were getting wed, but he was to say nothing yet. "I didn't think we'd be happy in London," I explained. "I'm looking for something less stressful until we get used to the idea of being together. I'm still aiming at Fleet Street, but a year out of the rat-race is the best plan."

"Yeah, that's more or less what Max thinks," he said casually, turning our chops out on to the plates. "He's hoping to talk you round, I believe."

Clairvoyance was a new line for my witty Brummie, but he was dead right. Max said in his funny way: "I've got used to you being around. If it's a question of money...."

"Thanks for that, Max, it isn't the money, and it will be a wrench leaving – I've learnt plenty here. It's just that now I've got to stop being a lone wolf and get used to being part of a couple."

Funnily enough, the captain of the Dogs' Home, possibly remembering the mass coverage I got them with the pussy-cat story, offered me a job as Public Relations Officer to the home. The American model of having a PR man in every firm was just beginning to catch on in the UK. It must have been the easiest publicity job ever – who in the world had not heard of the Battersea Dogs' Home?

And then there was that other novelty from the States – what the Press were pleased to describe as the Electronic Brain, aka the computer. I was still doing my industrial coverage, of course, and one of my company contacts said I should talk to a young electronic scientist for a possible story. I met the young prof a few days later and eventually did a story about his wonderful new machine that could do the work of 40 accountants in ten minutes, or something like that. As the papers, radio and TV caught on, I found myself acting as a liaison between my prof and the media. So it wasn't long before he offered me a job as PR man to his newborn company.

"I can't pay you much," he confessed, "but if you like we'll work out a deal whereby you get a stake in the company."

I thought this would be too risky and turned it down. Of course, I did, and of course I hardly need to tell you that his little baby is today part of one of the world's leading companies out there in America's Silicon Valley.

Meanwhile, Robina having lifted the ban on publicity, I was invited to meet her family for traditional Sunday lunch at their bungalow home in Catherington, a village between Portsmouth and Petersfield. Her Scottish father – 'Paw' they called him – was a Royal Navy war veteran as a yeoman of signals, at one time with Lord Louis Mountbatten. I was rather nervous about meeting him as he seemed a tough, old-fashioned guy who had led his local council for some years. A staunch Labour man.

"Och laddie," he said in his clear-cut Scottish way. "You were on the *News* then. Ye'll ken yon news editor Bill Wilkinson, then? He used to be ma next door neighbour – what did you make of him?"

Oh dear. This was more than awkward. What the hell could I say? "Frankly we were never on the best of terms...." I started.

Paw grinned broadly....and interrupted me:

"I hated the shifty bugger," he said.

The heads of his wife 'Maw', his other daughter Dee, and Robina, swivelled round and they stared at us both gobsmacked.

Maw turned out to be an absolute darling – the artistic younger daughter of the artist William Snape, one of Gosport's two Royal Academy brothers. I also met her fearsome older sister Auntie Kate, who merits a whole book on her own.

I'd been interviewed and accepted a reporter's job on the *Bath Evening Chronicle* known in the trade as the only country weekly that comes out every day. Says it all, really. The pay was 15 guineas a week, the same as I'd been getting on the *SLP*. Robina and I had looked at a few flats but settled for a mews flat (over stables converted to garages) at a former stately home which had re-mustered as the Combe Grove Hotel, a couple of miles from Bath city out on the edge of the beautiful Limpley Stoke Valley.

With my defection and Bowater, his other flatmate, also moving out to live with his intended, a pretty girl named Ursula, Trenbirth was clearly heartbroken. He talked of enlisting in the French Foreign Legion, but in fact landed on his feet among a bunch of similar ex-pat journalists on the *Halifax Courier* in Nova Scotia.

But he did come to our December wedding at St Jude's Church, Southsea (patron saint of lost causes, Robina said). Practically the entire reporting staff at the *News* were invited, outnumbering both families – which got us into a heap of future trouble from unforgiving aunts and cousins.

We settled into our flat at the Combe Grove for our week's honeymoon, going into the hotel to eat such meals as we bothered with: it boasted a famous chef and was home to the local Gourmet Club. After Christmas with Paw and Maw it was back to work, me at the *Chronicle* and Robina as a nurse at St. Martin's Hospital. I discovered from the news editor, Monty Pooley, that I was expected to cover the courts in the morning, have the afternoon much to myself, and do the evening jobs as they came up – Bath council, and the occasional opening night at the Bath Theatre Royal, my first being a show featuring the comic Sandy Powell (catchphrase "Can you hear me, Mother?")

The fly in the ointment was the hotel proprietor Mrs Christmas, a dumpy little woman with a phoney upper-class accent which manifested itself by dropping all the 'g's at the end of words, so that what you got was huntin', shootin' and fishin'. She ruled Combe Grove with a whiplash tongue, and that included her 'partner' whom she called 'Daddy' and who I reckon had a dog's life. Once, uncharacteristically, the hotel was full and she made the poor bugger sleep in her bath while she let his room.

The only exception was her brilliant chef who she spoiled rotten. The rest of the staff included the Jumblies, a set of overweight charladies from the surrounding hamlets, plus a genteel lady – a hard-luck case recruited from a gentlewomen's help society, who was on 'bread and board' and pitiful pocket money. This slave (and quite a few came and went in our time) lived a sort of 'spook' existence, carefully avoiding any guest. When she saw us, she scuttled off into some nether region in case Mrs Christmas accused her of 'gossip' and threatened to withhold a meal or two.

Robina, who was only working part-time, found herself being asked to help as a chambermaid (she confessed she actually liked this, snooping about among the guests' things) or kitchen hand, and I was sometimes seen down in the kitchens washing and preparing vegetables, too.

Mrs C also employed a gardener, Old Tom, a man in his fifties and of biblical proportions. He'd been a boy when the house was family-occupied. Chatting to him one day (he was the only one not scared of ''er Ladyship' as he called her), he told me: "Oo else is she gorna get to do what I do, for the pi'nce I gets?"

It was a fair point. He confided to me that he'd never been to London, and only twice in his life had he visited Bath, two miles down the road, just a threepenny bus-ride away.

We'd only been in the place a few days and were chatting to 'Daddy' in the hotel when a terrible scream came from the kitchen and the chef exploded onto the scene waving a cleaver. He gave another terrible scream, then rushed back to the kitchen shouting "Coffee, coffee!"

"I'd better make him a cup of coffee," 'Daddy' said calmly, and wandered off. When he returned he drew us into the bar. "Always have a bracer about this time of the morning," he told us. "Care to join me?"

The chef's somewhat flaky temperament never interfered with his cooking. He'd been the personal chef to some earl or duke, and had blotted his copybook, gradually descending down the chef ladder until landing on his feet with Mrs C, whose tenure at Combe Down depended on her gourmet society dinners and the hotel permanents. These included a retired admiral and his lady; Mr and Mrs the Hon Algernon; a retired Indian tea planter, and a 'solo' ex-public schoolmaster and uncle of a celebrated novelist who had never been near the place.

Uncle Rupert and I became friends when I solved, by sheer guesswork, a tricky clue in *The Times* crossword. He was writing a book about some esoteric period in Nelson's navy and asked if I might give him a hand sorting his stuff out. In return, he put down a cash deposit on a Smith Corona portable, with me paying the weekly instalments (sometimes).

Robina and I dined at the hotel at least once a week – we had done a deal for a set rate with Mrs C; the permanents had a similar deal going, so that the place would look busy when visitors dropped in. We were not allowed to eat in when the Gourmet Society came.

Mrs C's reputation was well-known around the villages and one night in the pub the butcher confessed that she had not paid him for three months. In fact most of the landowners around the place owed him money – the total I reckoned to be in the hundreds of pounds.

"Why don't you stop supplying them?" I asked. How naive.

"You don't know much about living in this sort of village," he said. "If I was to threaten that, they'd gang up on me and I wouldn't have any of them taking my meat. I couldn't live on the local trade, no matter how honest they are. Welcome to rural reality, mister."

Another rural reality was the farm neighbouring the hotel. It was run by a family of four – Mum, Dad and two hefty sons in their early 20s – with occasional hired-in help. It was mostly meat and dairy, with a fine herd of cows, and a small piggery backing onto the garden (mostly huge trees) behind our flat. Mark and Tony were amiable and we became pals. They both fell in love with Robina, of course, and treated her like visiting royalty. Their mum kept chickens and contributed to the home economy by marketing eggs and honey from the bees.

A typical incident cut the ice. I was strolling down to the farmhouse to get some eggs one day, when the mother came out and called: "Quick come in – the boys have got Rocky, the bull, out....hurry!"

I rushed up to the front door and she slammed it shut behind me. At this point I realised Robina was due home from work and I told Mary she was due to pass by any moment.

"Quick, go upstairs and keep lookout from the window – give her a shout to go straight to the hotel."

As Robina said later: "I saw you coming down the path, but you turned off to the farm. "Next thing I know, as I got level with the turning, you were hanging out of a bedroom window. Not good enough, I thought. Then I saw Rocky amble across the path into his paddock, followed by the boys."

Tony reckoned old Rocky had put in a full shift and was too tired to get awkward.

The boys could often be bucolic – they used to give us a call when they were bringing the boar, Errol, up to the sows in the piggery, in case we had visitors who might like to see the exciting events of mating. Talking of which reminds me....I arrived home one afternoon to be met by a 'Hello, Daddy' greeting from Robina. A bit of a shock. I sipped the glass of Scotch she handed me and we toasted the baby, and then each other. "Wipe the stupid grin off your face," she told me. We hugged, we laughed, and we cried.

"Are you sure?" I asked, the silly question every husband asks at least once.

"Confirmed by the village doctor," she said. "And he's offered me a part-time job as his receptionist, so he can keep an eye on me – I mean us, me and the babe."

Soon she also resigned her chambermaid duties, but agreed to help out on Sunday afternoons as a teatime waitress; tea and cream-cakes being offered as a treat for locals out for a walk. I used to drop in for tea and toast, with Mrs C's black cherry jam, a specialty the old monster imported from Switzerland. One afternoon, I was sitting reading *The Observer* at my usual seat behind the open door to the tea-room and Robina was busy the other side of the room. I heard the footsteps of a customer. "Well Hel-lo," he carolled across the floor. "The old place is looking up indeed. What's *your* name, angel?"

"Hello, zurr," I heard the 'angel' say. Suddenly she's developed a sort of Mummerset milkmaidy accent. I am just about to shove the door hard in his direction when she forestalls me.

"I'll be with 'ee zoon, zur. Just zoon's I've zerved this old gentleman over 'ere."

The newcomer moves into the room and sits down, a sturdy chap about my age, neat and military even in blazer and flannels. He glares at me. I glare back.

The Mummerset waitress returns with a pot of tea and a tray of cups and saucers, cake, and toast and jam. "My name's Robina," she says, thankfully in her normal voice." And this is my husband, John."

I am obliged to stick my hand out, and he, embarrassed, quickly seizes it and shakes it warmly.

"Craig," he says.

He turned out to be a captain in the Royal Marines, wounded in Malaya, and home on leave. We became firm friends and took to joy-riding around in his car, visiting the local pubs and helping to line him up with girlfriends. It wasn't too difficult.

At the *Bath Chronicle*, I got so bored I grew a beard – a full set trimmed in a style called 'The Imperial'. Very appropriate because it was the name of the premier hotel in Bath. The paper, even though a daily, was somewhat over-staffed. We reporters (Gerry Goodman, Ian Todd, George Gordon, a young girl called Tina, and a newcomer named Phillips-Mugglestone) worked for a news editor, Monty Pooley, and there was also a chief reporter, Ken Goodman. The Goodman brothers were from nearby Trowbridge, where they had made a name for themselves as district reporters and were well-acquainted with my Uncle George, brewmaster at Ushers of Trowbridge. George Gordon was to go on to win himself a good reputation in Fleet Street and Ian Todd also scored as a top-notch rugby reporter.

Put it this way, I don't remember ever having to work in the afternoons. Evenings yes, there were council meetings to cover, theatre opening nights, local am-dram, a fairly busy schedule – but since Mr Pooley and the Goodmans liked to grab anything that might offer lineage possibilities, or free drinks, not too much of this came my way.

Court-cover most mornings made up much of my workload, but there were only a few good stories. The first was when I was covering the magistrates court and they put an old tramp in the box, the sort that you might have met in *Punch* cartoons in the 1930s: shabby overcoat, frayed trouser bottoms, dented top hat and a crummy choker. He was accused of stealing roses from the corporation display in the park, to the value of 1s 6d.

He pleaded guilty and was then asked by the clerk if he had anything to say in mitigation. This was explained to him as 'something that would explain why he did it.' I can see in my mind's eye the poor old sod standing there in front of those well-fed magistrates: "I wanted to give them to the pretty ladies of Bath," he said, "in memory of my mother."

Instead of giving him a week in a warm cell, the idiots fined him 10 shillings. Where did they think he was going to get the money? Perhaps they were street-savvy enough to know that John Donaldson of the *Bristol Post* and Dick Ledbury, the Bath freelance, would be slipping him a few bob, along with yours truly – plus the pound or so the court copper rounded up among his mates.

I also covered the County Court sessions – the civil court – and one morning when the pressure was on at Bath Guildhall, where Quarter Sessions and magistrates courts were taking up the space, the County Court was relegated to a cramped chamber, hastily fitted up with a tall desk and a few rows of chairs. I was sitting at the tiny Press table practically underneath the Judge's Bench when His Honour took his seat. First off he leaned over and asked if I was the Press, and told me to open my notebook. He then launched into a ferocious attack on the City of Bath for their ignorance of judicial protocol.

"The office of Judge of the County Court is the oldest judicial position in the land," he said. "These ignorant officials have seen fit to ignore this and have filled their courtrooms with Quarter Sessions proceedings and even magistrates courts, while I am removed to this cramped, ill-lit chamber without so much as an apology. I would not be surprised if they are not severely reprimanded by the Lord Chief Justice of this land."

He then leaned over and raised an eyebrow at me. I nodded.

"I shall now adjourn this court for....(pause for another glance at me) for 20 minutes."

I nodded again – 20 minutes would be fine for me to sell the story to the *Daily Mail*.

The Royal beard

There was a further incident involving the Guildhall a little later. The burghers of Bath had made some alterations to the old building and also, I recall, the famous Abbey in the city centre. No less a figure than Queen Elizabeth, the Queen Mother, was invited to perform the honours at an inaugural ceremony at the Guildhall. As is the custom at such events in order to limit the number of Press reporters and photographers, the rota system was applied, which meant that a single reporter would cover part of an event and share the story with other media later.

As it happened I was the duty man chosen for an outside spot at the side of the Abbey where the Royal visitor was to lead a small ceremony, unveiling a plaque after she'd had a tour of the building. After watching the Queen Mother arrive and wave to the crowds before going into the Guildhall, I nipped round the side to take up my position. A couple of local bobbies were stationed some way behind me to keep the crowds of well-wishers behind the barriers.

There was the usual lengthy wait and I gradually moved up closer to the side door of the Guildhall. Eventually there was the sound of conversation inside and then a bit of a commotion: someone banged on the inside of the door, which had obviously become stuck. My natural reaction was to grab the door handle and pull: the door swung back and the poor Queen Mum was literally pitched forward almost into my arms, more than somewhat startled....

I leapt back a pace, stood to attention, and said: "Oops, sorry, Ma'am."

"Ah, the Press," she said, recovering quickly. "For a moment I thought you were King George, my father-in-law. It's the beard, you see." Then with that engaging smile, she moved swiftly on as only a practised Royal can.

Next day I shaved the beard off and never grew it again.

Chronicle reporters didn't very often find themselves covering unexpected, off-diary events. But I was loafing about the office one morning after a short session at the courts, when Garth, our photographer, stuck his head round the door.

"Interested in a story?" he asks. "Only there's a bullock escaped from the market. Running amok in the town centre."

We nip off towards the shops, and indeed, the bullock decides to give us a neat headline by wandering into....a china shop. Garth gets busy trying to get a picture of the animal against a background of smashed china, of which there is plenty. I'm outside talking to the shop girls.

"Look out, he's coming out," someone shouts and Garth and I back out fast.

The bullock heads off through the side streets in the direction of the recreation ground and we follow. He leads us a merry dance up towards the rec, well ahead of us, and then rushes off down the lane, past some cottages and through an open gate into a field.

Garth nips in and takes a quick photograph of the animal, now calmly munching grass, while I watch. Then he gets a sniff of us and decides to get to know us better. I take off fast for the gate, nip through and slam it shut.

"Oh my God, I've left Garth in there!"

But as I frame the thought, Garth comes flying over the five-bar gate, still bravely clutching his camera.

"Bloody idiot! I was trapped in there," he says. I think he was a bit stressed....

In fact, we'd lost the bullock. He somehow got out of that field and re-appeared near the Theatre Royal, where a police marksman put him down with one neat shot. Garth and I got a fair spread in the paper, but we agreed over a couple of pints that we were sorry they'd killed our playful chum.

Bath was one of those places that was given more prominence than its size deserved. For instance, it had its own constabulary with a full-blown Chief Constable and Deputy Chief Constable. I was introduced to them early on and I am bound to say it was something of an experience. The chief was a dapper little bloke from South London, cock-sparrow accent and all. He was delighted to learn I'd worked there. We swapped reminiscences of The Cornet of Horse of Course – and of mutual acquaintants in the Met. The deputy, on the other hand, was a caricature of the country copper: big, beefy and with a farmer's ruddy face, and a drawling West Country delivery. These two unlikely companions revelled in an entertaining double act (their bobbies called them Laurel and Hardy behind their backs) that actually hid two very shrewd brains in perfect harmony and Bath was well up the league-table for crime clear-up rates. Robina and I met them one day at Bath races, where we had a very jolly time and came home with money in our pockets.

Talking of money in our pockets: Robina had been shopping in town one morning and we met for lunch.

"Look at this," she said, holding out her shopping basket. "I'd just paid for the veg but as I was leaving, the greengrocer stuck this pineapple in....'just a little gift from me,' he said, 'How's John getting on, by the way?'"

"Ah," I told her. "You don't remember meeting him, do you .. at the wrestling. He promotes the shows – he's just making sure of his publicity in the *Chronicle*."

It was one of those evening jobs that used to come my way. I'd taken her along: it wasn't her kind of entertainment, she said. But she did enjoy the pineapple.

Animals played a big part in our life at Bath – and not just on the farm. Combe Down Hotel, with its orangery backed by an extensive lawn and superb views over the valley below, was a very popular place for wedding receptions. Of course, that meant staff to wait on the guests – and here Robina and I (and even some of the 'permanents') were leaned on to help out. One marvellous summer's day (all the more marvellous since the season was actually a very damp one in the West Country), the bride was in her perfect white dress, the groom in his tailored suit, the lady guests all vying with each other in lacy finery and the men dressed as gentry. On the lawn, the flunkies moved discreetly around the groups of guests, the fluting voices and tinkling laughter as the champagne fizzed in their glasses drifting across the grounds.

The father of the bride takes a swig, clears his throat ready to make his speech, and....(enter stage left) Sophie, the very pregnant sow from the piggery, snorting and trumpeting and heading straight for the buffet. Very fond of a vol-au-vent was Sophie, or anything else that could broadly be defined as edible – by her, that is. Cue screams from the other females, shrieks and nifty footwork as the bridesmaids head for the hills. A protective group forms around the bride, who is having hysterics.

Mrs C is pointing at any male within range and screaming: "Don't just stand there! Chase her away...."

All the shouting and screaming finally deflects Sophie from the trough (or buffet), and she heads back towards the open door of the orangery. Some brave men head her off and she runs for the trees. At this point the brothers from next door, Mark and Tony, come rushing up with a long pole, followed by Tom the gardener. He shows an amazing turn of speed as Sophie seems to recognise him and charges after him as he turns away. Trumpeting loudly, she butts him playfully and he sprawls across her back....

"Hold her there, Tom!" shouts Tony. But Tom's clinging on for life and the drag of his body pulls Sophie off-course so that they wheel round in circles. I'm impressed at how quickly Mrs C, Robina. and the other ladies vanish off the face of the earth.

The combined weight of Sophie and Tom (now with his arms round her neck) crashes into the buffet tables, one of which collapses, showering pig and gardener with paper plates of vols-au-vent and sausage rolls. Eating and trampling over the fodder, in what may well be an act of cannibalism on her part, Sophie concentrates on the grub.

Tony eventually leads her away. I suddenly remember I'm supposed to be 'out on a job' and disappear.

On my work-free afternoons I used to walk out across the fields to meet Robina on her way home from her shift at the doctor's. Every now and then, we'd have to make a wide detour to avoid going anywhere near the quarry on the hill sloping down from the village.

They used to hang out red flags and 'Danger – Blasting in Progress' signs all over the footpaths. It prompted Robina to say:

"It's not boring being married to you. So far I've been sold into slavery as an unpaid chambermaid; had to flee for my life from an angry bull; been threatened with being dynamited to kingdom come....and I'm going to have a baby next month."

Chapter Nineteen
Life on the Wire

As the summer of 1960 faded, I realised our idyll on a small-town newspaper had to end. We were to be a family now: it was time to move on and earn real money – that, of course, meant moving back to London.

The Pompey Mafia led by Michael Gabbert was still in place, but the focus had shifted. Michael was now a sub-editor for the American Associated Press – The AP – in London. He'd also found jobs there for Phil Griffiths and Alan Biggs, another *News* district man. The AP was a big news agency that gathered stories from staff and 'stringers' around the globe, selling them on a subscription basis to newspapers, radio and television.

"Your timing always was spot on," he said when I called him. "Don McNichol, a Scot, is in charge of the 'domestic desk' and there is a vacancy. It's yours if you want it."

The pay worked out at exactly twice what I was getting in Bath. And there were opportunities to add to that, by working extra shifts. We would certainly need the extra – once Robina had the baby she would not be able to work. And that time was fast approaching. I gave the *Chronicle* the required month's notice and the deal was that, once the baby was delivered, Robina would go home to stay with her parents at their bungalow in Catherington, while I sorted out the flat I'd found in Finchley, North London.

One night, when I'd been up to London with some of our gear, and Robina had been at work, I'd arrived back at Combe Down around midnight. As I got to our front door, the phone was ringing – and I nearly wrecked the door trying to get my key to work. I grabbed the receiver.

"Hello Mr Bull and congratulations, you are the father of a bonny girl," chirruped our irrepressible doctor. "She's fine, he added, "but she had a tough time of it, so we've put her to sleep for a while. Best thing is if you come in about nine in the morning."

I've often felt guilty in my life – it tends to come with some aspects of the job – but never like I felt that September morn. I still shudder at the thought.

Robina was propped up in bed, cuddling a tiny, dark-haired creature with big eyes. But my God, my poor wife looked spectral. Her skin was damn near transparent and her great big eyes were shockingly bloodshot.

"Don't say anything, love." I leaned over and kissed her softly, hardly daring to touch her.

It transpired that she turned out to be what they called a 'bleeder' – a family trait that no-one had thought it necessary to mention.

While mother and baby stayed in hospital, waiting to move in with Maw and Paw, I went to work at the AP's modern offices at the end of Farringdon Street, round the corner from Fleet Street.

My hunt for a flat in London had not been easy – rents had soared in the year I'd been away, thanks to the Tory government lifting controlled-rent rules. I recall queuing literally for hours on the stairs of poky agents' offices in shabby rundown buildings in Clapham or Swiss Cottage. Often when I went to look at a flat, I was shocked by the appalling state it was in – no place to take a baby – and often not much under £20 a week. And the landlord, or more usually landlady, was often downright insulting. Once I was even turned away by a seriously hateful old cow near Swiss Cottage tube.

"Well I certainly can't take people like you," she told me at the door, "but I dare say you'll find someone who isn't so fussy about Jews."

Finally I got lucky with a very nice apartment; in a two-storey private block off Finchley High Road and handy for Finchley Central tube. It was built round three sides of a square, about 30 flats in all, backing onto a lane leading to a small park. Our flat was on the first floor, furnished, with a main bedroom, a child's bedroom, bathroom, kitchenette and sitting room. We even had our own patch of garden at the back – which had Robina dancing about with delight. We used to spend a lot of time knocking it into shape and laying out a vegetable plot, watched by little Yolanda propped up in her chair, gurgling and waving her chubby little arms about.

She was a remarkably co-operative baby, never fussy about her food. I recall her in the early months sitting in her high chair, picking up her mashed food by the handful and plastering it all over her face as she shoved it into her mouth. This seemed to me to be a good idea – and I even tried it myself, shoving a mouthful in with my fist and chomping away happily. Robina even joined in a couple of times.

Robina's nursing training advocated giving babies real food very early on. She and I used to pre-chew pieces of meat to feed to our little daughter from the age of about three months. This system was also popular with the other mothers around us. It turned out that our little 'estate' was home to a number of ex-pat Australians – young families whose husbands were interns completing their medical training at the famous London teaching hospitals, most of the wives being nurses like Robina.

It meant that we had a flourishing baby-sitting service, day or night, so that we were able to get out and about in London. Often, as the day warmed up, we took Yolanda down the lane to the little park, where she amused herself rolling about on the grass with the other babes, and desperately crawling after the bigger ones who were learning to walk.

Meanwhile, under the guidance of McNichoI, I gradually got on top of the job. We worked shifts – day shifts, night shifts and swing shifts, which were from afternoon through to midnight. This meant that the only time I saw the old Pompey Mafia – Michael Gabbert, Phil Griffiths and Alan Biggs – was at shift changeover time, or in the pub for a quick drink, because there was only ever one sub-editor per shift on the domestic desk. The news came in from around the world by telephone, by telegram or via the teleprinter: my job was to sub the copy (or rewrite it) as it arrived, bashing out the final version on a typewriter or pencilling-in corrections on the original. Often it was a case of 'translating' American into English, or correcting the English of foreign nationals. I then gave my copy to the skilled teleprinter operator (in those days, always a man) and it would be sent down the wire to our customers – the Fleet Street papers, other UK-based dailies and the BBC.

The London operation included writers who covered UK stories, as well as Continental and Middle Eastern news: in addition to British foreign correspondents, there were a number of 'star' American newsmen. The sports-desk reporters were generally British and covered football, cricket, tennis, golf and horse-racing. The whole operation was controlled by the cable editor, sitting in the hot-seat in the middle of the spider's web of reporters, who were sending copy out, and the domestic desk sub-editors who were rewriting incoming copy.

The AP were profligate in small things – for instance, a girl would come round at the start of every shift handing out freshly sharpened pencils – an apocryphal story in the AP magazine about a San Francisco cable editor's retirement said that his wife collected up every pencil she could find in the house and sent them (several hundred) back to the office in a small van.

I often worked with a teleprinter operator called Jan and we devised a system for improving our accuracy rate. He would clock every spelling mistake I made, and I would do the same for his typing. At a penny for each mistake, we started out handing over enough for a couple of pints in The Grapes, but in the end we both smartened up our act just to save money.

The overall boss of the outfit was John Lloyd, a quick-thinking New Yorker. On my first day he told me: "Now we use first names around here, so we both call each other John. Don, over there, tells me you are one of the bright boys from Portsmouth, sorry 'Pompey' as you guys apparently call the place. I look forward to reading your stuff – good luck, John."

I'd arrived at the AP just at the 1960 US election was warming up, culminating in an orgy of stories around John F Kennedy's popular win for the Democrats. We were expected to monitor what the Yanks called 'The Play' that our bulletins had been given by Fleet Street.

Typically, a report read like this:

AP showed well in headliners on Kennedy's Berliner speech. Reaction comment saw UP and INS picking up, but AP led well in Scan points.

Which meant:

Associated Press stories about Kennedy's Berliner speech were well-used in the press. United Press and International News Service, our rival agencies, got the follow-up stories but we led well in the Scandinavian media.

New York was always watching and was quick to find fault, though was always careful to 'talk' to us by teleprinter in their idea of Britspeak:

'I say chaps, can one of you give us a brief description of a 'panga'?'

Gabbert's reply: 'Panga: sharp, wide-bladed knife, useful in jungle or for murdering white Bwana. Very nasty.'

The Americans on the London beat included a couple of colourful newsmen who'd made their names as young men in World War II, genial guys like Eddie Gilmore and Tom Ochiltre, completely at home with the famous. Indeed Gilmore had been on buddy terms with Ernest Hemingway and Ed 'Goodnight and Good Luck' Murrow.

Eddie Gilmore treated us humble sub-editors as equals and

enthusiastically joined in our darts competitions at The Grapes, which was as near as we got to a canteen, apart from late-night bowls of super-soup (you could stand the spoon up in it) from The Soup Kitchen around the corner in Shoe Lane – "hungry newsmen and printers – a specialty."

A few years earlier, Eddie had made the news himself in his dealings with Stalin. In the course of his job he'd met and fallen in love with a Russian girl, Tania, and married her. However, relations between the US and the Soviet Union in the Cold War meant that it wasn't possible for Tania to leave Russia. Eddie had several US politicians and other international movers-and-shakers on the case – and Stalin himself became personally involved in the tug-of-war over Eddie's lovely bride. It became a *cause célèbre* in the world's media – until Eddie picked up a whisper that Russia was desperately short of ice-breaker ships. He started talks with US shipping interests and finally cooked up a deal: he swapped an ice-breaker from Alaska for his bride.

The story went round the world and Eddie wrote a book about it entitled *Troika* (the word for a Russian sledge drawn by three horses). Even then he got lucky, because the word gained global currency when used by the canny Russian leader Krushchev, who changed the idea of The West vs The Soviet Union by introducing the concept of the Third World, to include developing nations, which he called – Troika.

I saw how these American correspondents operated and made up my mind that's what I wanted to do. There were a couple of British AP chaps working abroad covering the violent upheavals in the former Belgian Congo. Thanks to the Belgian rule, the principal language in the Congo was French, which I spoke well enough to get by. I mentioned my interest to John Lloyd who seemed amenable to the idea: a precedent had recently been set by the despatch of Pat, a Brit from the American desk, to Stanleyville to help out. It wasn't somewhere you could take a wife and child, so Pat had gone alone and his wife occasionally used to drop in to the office in the evening, on the off-chance of being able to chat to her husband by phone or teleprinter.

I explained all this to Robina, stressing of course the sort of money the Americans paid their correspondents. She wasn't over the moon about it – the Congo was a war zone after all – but she'd known what she was taking on when she married a reporter. So, imagine how upset I was to learn that, instead of sending me to Stanleyville, the vacancy was being filled by some 23-year-old newcomer from the New York office (who turned out to be someone's nephew, of course).

In a fit of pique, I walked round the corner to the London office of the Agence France Presse, the French news agency, and asked for a job. There was a vacancy for a translator/sub-editor in their Paris office. Taking this as a good omen to start my foreign correspondent career, and after a discussion with Robina (unlike the Congo job, Robina and baby Yolanda would be able to come with me to Paris), I was given an appointment to come in and take a test.

JOHN BULL LEAVES ENGLAND
• LONDON—Most appropriately, this bureau had a staffer named John Bull. But he resigned recently to move to Paris.

21

How the AP's staff magazine broke the news of my departure

A week later, having worked a full shift for them with no obvious cock-ups, I was told they'd take me on.

Chapter Twenty
Rue St Lazare

It was a beautiful early summer and I took a holiday, having given a month's notice to the AP. Robina, who was expecting again, was glad of the break and we spent an idyllic couple of weeks by the sea with our daughter Yolanda, meanwhile brushing up on our French.

At the end of June I flew to Paris alone to arrange a flat and to go through the bureaucratic formalities. The offices of the Agence France Press (AFP) were down in the *deuxième arrondissement,* near the Bourse, the Paris stock exchange. Thanks (again) to the Pompey Mafia connection with *The People,* I met up with Henry Khan, their man in Paris. Now it just so happened that a magazine belonging to *The People's* owners, Odhams Press, had just decided to withdraw its Paris correspondent, who had been living in a flat on the Rue St Lazare. The rent, moreover, had been paid for the next three months – wonderful – because at 66,000 francs a month (half my £35-per-week salary) there was no way that I could have afforded it.

Henry took me to inspect the flat on the corner of the Rue des Martyrs leading up to Montmartre and the gleaming white church of Sacré Coeur. A short walk in the other direction took me to Notre Dame de la Lorette and the Metro for the Bourse, with only one change on the way. The flat itself, on the second floor, was small but nicely arranged with French windows in the sitting room looking out onto Rue St Lazare, one small bedroom with just about room for Yolanda's cot, and a miniscule kitchen and bathroom. It would actually suit Robina very well – there wasn't much to keep clean and tidy.

I went through some complex, bureaucratic formalities with my new boss, Monsieur Jacques Lapine, director of the English desk. This included obtaining a *Police Judiciaire* card which all citizens had to carry. And having a medical. This involved me in taking all my clothes off, and, on the signal of a bulb lighting up, to walk through an interior door into a completely dark room. A disembodied voice instructed me to turn left, to turn right, head up, head down, bend down – and so (embarrassingly) on....

The AFP, as an employer, was very socially minded. Monsieur Lapine explained that I would have medical insurance paid by the company; wages were based on a 13-month year, which gave us all a month's pay as a Christmas bonus; and because Robina was English, she would initially have the services of an experienced Parisienne to help her through the mysteries of shopping and other social arrangements.

My immediate boss on the English desk was American, an amiable black guy called Bill, who spoke an attractive mixture of polite French and New York slang. Above him in the hierarchy was our chief sub-editor, a formidable Scottish woman in her fifties, known only as 'Mac.' Just like the one I'd left behind in Blighty.

Here's a sample dialogue:

Mac: *"Ça va pour les Scan points, mon gars....mais pour les autres...."*

Bill: *"D'accord, Mac,* but let's shift *les Scan assez vite – et les* extreme orient *plus tard."*

It was surprising how quickly I got the hang of this kind of communication. What often threw us, however, was the proximity of half a dozen subs apparently having a mutiny at the next desk.

"That's the Italians," Bill explained. "It's just the way they are. Nothin' we can do but live with it."

During my first days Monsieur Lapine took a keen interest in my work. One story I'd spiked caught his attention: "Why didn't you run this?" he asked, holding up my spiked copy. "It's Kennedy's New Jersey speech."

"Sure it's Kennedy," I said, "but he's not saying anything new – he's not changed his positon on Cuba one iota."

He tutted a bit.

"But he's the President of the United States," he protested.

"Sure. But everyone knows he's the President – it's not news and neither is this speech. If we put out every utterance, whether it was relevant or not, we'd fill the wires with words: just words, instead of news."

Lapine walked away looking thoughtful. I had shown him something that had been brought home to me at the American Associated Press. But I wasn't sure I'd be able to convince the French – after all, the AFP was part-supported by the French government and they probably liked 'empty air' speeches.

Actually the world's media was much more interested in Paris itself. The political battle, between those who wanted to hold on to the French colony in Algeria and those that didn't, had taken a pretty ugly turn. The Algerian freedom-fighters, the FLN, had been fighting the French army for years, but recently they'd taken the fight into the streets of Paris, targeting cops especially. President De Gaulle, who had taken power for himself a year earlier in what was essentially a coup d'état, was flirting with the idea of ending the conflict by giving the Algerians independence. This, of course, brought a revolt among the so-called *Pieds Noirs*, the French settlers very much established in the colony. The campaign against De Gaulle's police had become a growing ulcer in the struggle for and against independence.

Most people, including me, thought that it was going to blow over. In July I returned to London to bring Robina and Yolanda, and a huge pile of luggage, out to Paris. We arrived on a stinking hot day at the Gare du Nord accompanied by nine different pieces of luggage, Yolanda's cot and pushchair, and the various necessities of travel including a vacuum flask of cold water. Robina, now five months' pregnant, flaked out on a bench while I organised porters and a cab to take us home. When I got back to the bench, I discovered the flask had been stolen from her bag. Welcome to Paris.

Determined to make the best of it, we were pleased with the romance of our little Parisian home and Yolanda discovered the delights of sailing little paper boats in the bidet. We hardly ever closed the French doors onto out tiny balcony, with a view of a fruit and flower stall beneath us in the rue. I often took Yolanda in her pushchair up through the carnival atmosphere of the Rue des Martyrs. One morning, as we climbed up the hill, she began gurgling with excitement and pointing at something coming up behind me. I turned to look – and did a classic 'double skull'. Lolloping up the rue behind me was a seven-foot tall brown bear, dancing to a tin whistle played by its keeper. After that, every time we went out Yolanda kept looking right and left, expecting other giant Teddies to show up to play with her.*

---

* Yolanda actually had to wait about ten years (and suffer quite a lot of leg-pulling from the family) for her faith to be justified. We were on holiday in St Malo: turning a corner, we ran slap into....a beautiful brown bear, nobly strolling down the street, on a lead just like a pet dog. She was righteously smug about that. Still is.

Robina and I took her with us when we went for an enjoyable haggle with the stallholders along the Rue des Martyrs on our way to Montmartre and Sacré Coeur and she loved the little funicular that carried a coachload of people up and down like a miniature cablecar. Robina preferred the views from the balcony opposite the 'white sepulchre' of the great church itself. Yolanda was disappointed, I'm afraid, with our local park, Le Parc Monceau. I'd taken her over there one afternoon to give Robina a chance to take it easy. I was sitting on a bench with my daughter playing happily on the grass when a large *flic* approached, swinging his baton in my direction.

None of your courteous British bobby here: "Take that child off the grass," he ordered roughly. Apparently no-one was allowed on the grass, not even toddlers.

"Where can she play?" I asked.

"Pouf!" he said, dismissing this foreigner for his ignorance. "In the sand pit, of course."

"But she'll try to eat it," I protested. He gave me a narrow-eyed look and touched the pistol on his belt....and I grabbed Yolanda and took off for new pastures. I regarded this incident as something of an omen – and as it happened, I was right to do so.

As promised, Robina's shopping guide showed up to take her to the *grands magasins* on the boulevards, and Henry Khan phoned to suggest a drink. Incidentally we had a TURbigo phone number, something much prized by the locals, in the same way that a FLAxman number was snobbishly over-valued in London (in those days, you dialled the first three letters before the number). Henry dropped a titbit he'd heard – 13 policemen had been murdered in Paris the week before, something that had not been reported in the media. A lot of things were not reported in the media at this time, especially a number of *manifs* (short for *manifestations* – what we call 'demonstrations') in the suburbs which had turned violent: there were even some nasty mob scenes on the Champs Elysées.

Then came some personal bad news. The AFP arranged for Robina to have a maternity examination with a specialist doctor near the park and we were both impressed by the obviously upmarket practice. I waited impatiently in an ante room while she had a lengthy consultation. The doctor came out looking very grave – apparently the baby was lying awkwardly in the womb and it would be a difficult birth. Being a nurse, Robina knew exactly what this meant and explained it to me. She seemed to think the doctor was making too much of it, but I certainly didn't agree. The doctor's secretary gave me a written report for my employers, which I duly handed over to Monsieur Lapine. He read it with great care, his face growing longer as he did so.

"Well," he finally said, "this is a blow. You were getting on pretty well here...."

"What d'you mean?"

"Well, *mon ami*, you do realise that we are in a Roman Catholic country, don't you? The excellent nursing sisters at the maternity hospital often tend to believe they should save the baby....if it should come to a choice," he gently added. "Believe me, John, I don't want to lose you – but in your shoes I should get my wife into an English hospital when the time comes."

He suggested I take a few days to think it over, but I knew I wasn't going to risk losing my Robina, despite her insisting that she was ready to stay on.

"Or I could go home to have the baby, then come back," she said. "I'm feeling perfectly okay."

"No. We are going back. It isn't worth the risk. I'll tell Lapine in the morning."

Within a few days, as the violence on the streets – led by the outlawed *Organisation de l'Armée Secret (OAS)* – increased, an incident convinced me. I was walking back from Notre Dame de la Villette after my day-shift when a couple of lorryloads of riot cops arrived and set up roadblocks either end of the street. Several teams of para-militaries started lining people up against the walls.

"Passport," demanded an ugly-looking heavy, pushing me back against the wall. I fished out my Press card and showed it. He snatched it from my hand and threw it in the gutter.

"I said 'Passport!'" he screamed in my face, with a thump in the guts with the butt of his automatic rifle.

I managed to get my passport out and handed it over.

"Thought so – a foreigner," he said contemptuously. "Come with me." He pulled my arm as I bent to retrieve my Press card and shoved me up the street to the barrier. A senior officer then took my passport and Press card and examined them carefully, consulting a list of presumably 'wanted' men.

"Go home and try to stay out of trouble," he told me, waving me away.

I wasn't hurt, but the over-reaction from the soldiers and gendarmes showed just how jumpy they were.

The next day I cleared my desk, bade farewell to Bill and Mac, and went to lunch with Monsieur Lapine, who handed over our air-tickets to London. I took them straight to the Air France office and cashed them in. Then I went to the Gare du Nord and bought tickets for the boat train through to Waterloo. On Friday morning we said farewell to Madame La Concierge and took a cab to the station. It was then September and among our packages was Yolanda's first birthday present – a toy dachshund to remind her of Paris.

At Waterloo, with Robina pushing Yolanda in her buggy, I negotiated with a porter – money changed hands and he produced a sort of cage on wheels, loaded our nine pieces of luggage aboard, and transferred it to the goods van. I've never been more pleased to see my in-laws when our taxi from Petersfield arrived at their bungalow at Catherington.

Chapter Twenty One
Kings and Emperors

Before I went to Paris, Michael Gabbert had the bright idea of setting up a freelance agency in the *Evening News* circulation area, to take advantage of the fact that *News* reporters were paid not to do lineage. He made it clear that he and I would merely invest in the venture – Phil Griffiths was keen to run it, along with another Pompey mafia reporter, Brian Northeast. They would have modest pay and expenses, and in return they would be given shares in the outfit as it grew. I was interested in this long-term sideline, but of course I had no spare money: after some haggling, it was decided that my contribution would be my motorbike for the reporters to use, and I would also take care of some other up-front expenses such as typewriters and so on.

The official launch of Hampshire News Service (HNS) was celebrated by the four of us having a decent lunch in the upstairs dining-room at Schmidts in London's Charlotte Street and toasting the start of the venture with cigars and vintage port.

"See us kings and emperors carving up the best bits of Europe," said Michael, whose history was colourful but somewhat lacking in accuracy.

Michael had recently come into some money, so had rented an office for the News Service near the law courts in Winchester, and put down the deposit on a bungalow for Northeast and his wife, who would then pay rent towards the mortgage repayments. The scheme had started well: Michael was able to use the HNS for exclusive stories for *The People* (or even follow up stories lifted from the *Evening News*). *The People*, incidentally, were paying up to £300 a time for exclusives – an unheard-of figure at the time.

So when I returned to England in September – out of a job – I had, at least, the opportunity to work for the agency. The plot was that Robina would stay with her parents until the baby was born and I would give her most of my earnings. In the event, Brian Northeast wanted to leave the agency and was fixed up with a job in the Manchester office of *The People* and Phil elected to return to the American Associated Press.

One of the problems had been that, when we sold a good story, we had to get photos – which meant giving the photographer the lion's share of the fee. So I hired in a freelance just returned from the US and looking for work – a genuine beatnik called Harold

– accompanied by his girlfriend, a crazy New Yorker of Russian background, who called herself Thelma. They were a lot of fun and would do anything, very cheaply. We found we could even afford to add a small darkroom at the office where Thelma could do the work and save on fees, and to pay for the petrol for Harold's Ford car. I moved into Michael's empty home rent-free, which enabled me to send a reasonable amount of money every week back to Robina.

Later we found another lost soul, Simon Regan – a nearly-normal young man who had been thrown out of most countries in Europe: he had lived in Finland among the Lapps, who had given him a young teenage girl to 'look after'. He was naive enough to try to enter Germany with this companion – and was lucky merely to be deported to England. Once, I asked him to show me his passport: it fell to pieces as I opened it. Most pages had a police stamp with '*Verboten*' or the equivalent prominently displayed. Regan was hired on slave wages while he learned the trade and was given my motorbike to run around on. Abetted by Harold, he set about making connections in the world of astral-plane pyscho nutters and began selling stories to outfits like *Psychic News* and some of the more esoteric weekly papers.

Amazingly, the money started to roll in. My biggest contribution was resurrecting stories I had covered in my days in south-east Hampshire and re-running them – for instance, the story of Bill Botting, the blind tobacconist, who could tell his customers by voice and footfall.

"Good morning, Bill," I said. "I'll give you a clue. I've come to talk to you about the guy who robbed you a few years back."

"Ah, thought it sounded like you," he said. "You still on the *News* then?" And we took it from there.

The Agency did a deal with Fleet Street's *Daily Sketch* where the *Sketch* sponsored the historic Guy Fawkes celebrations in Winchester. King Alfred's teacher training college in the city organised the festivities, and colleges all around the area joined in by making huge effigies of politicians and showbiz stars, with us handling the publicity. We also hit the front pages of every popular paper with a story of the British Army recruiting young men by advertising on beermats....and we sold a big story to *The People* about a medium whose spirit-guide from beyond the grave, her soldier boyfriend killed in World War II, got in touch by pinging her stocking suspenders.

When the Minister of War, John Profumo, was due to arrive by helicopter at the barracks in Winchester, we sent Harold out to buy clothes more suitable to cover a formal event. He showed up with an evening dress suit, shiny from wear, and I had to ask Regan to take him back and get something less ridiculous.

We got orders from Fleet Street's finest to cover a gypsy funeral, featuring the cremation of the matriarch in her caravan. Harold's pictures of this event went round the world, including a famous shot of the village vicar, in full fig, walking down a country lane with the local bobby, a superb contrast in black and white.

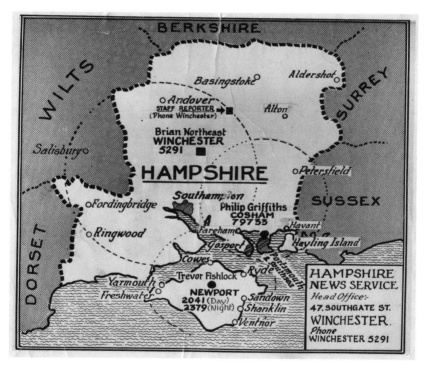

Our freelance agency - 'covers Hampshire like the dew'

So the money was coming in nicely, but the trouble was, we didn't know when to stop expanding. For instance, we'd offered a deal to Trevor Fishlock, who after his training on the *News*, had set himself up as a freelance on the Isle of Wight. Newspapers and magazines would pay us for his work each month, and we would pay him a regular wage, if necessary making up any shortfall. This was good for Trevor, but a disaster for us because we forgot to cream off *any* of the money he made over and above his wages, but always remembered to make good any shortfalls. In other words, we were bound to lose out. Instead of learning from this mistake, we also took on a girl reporter to cover the area north of Winchester on similar terms.

Expenses soon began to take over the cash-flow: the office rent, the expenses of running Harold's car and his rented flat, began to overwhelm us. We tried to earn more by recruiting Bob Perrin, also ex-*News*, who was working as a freelance for the *Sunday Pictorial* – an early attempt at celebrity news. But this quickly became uneconomic, as he was expected to find stories in the clubs and upmarket pubs of Southsea: his memberships and bar bills were astronomical.

Robina's cash dropped down to about £12 a week by the time she was booked into a nursing home at Liss, near Petersfield, for the birth, due in November.

Perrin and I managed to keep the rent paid for the office, but only by sneaking the typewriters out of the back door and selling them to a secondhand shop. Other bits of gear started to go, too. Harold and Thelma did a moonlight flit from their flat, and Harold had been streetwise enough to take all of the negatives with him. They were his copyright, of course, and even years after the event, some of these pictures were still showing up in the magazine press.

The crash didn't hurt too much. Bob disappeared to London and the BBC, Trevor and our girl in Andover resumed freelancing, Regan found a job in Banbury and never looked back....and Michael rented out the bungalow, just covering his mortgage. He and I agreed that we'd learnt some useful lessons. Ever afterwards we could walk into anyone's offices and instantly know if they were on the skids. Been there – know what it smells like.

I jumped on my faithful Franny Barnett motorbike, rode over to the *Daily Echo* office in Southampton and asked to see the editor. Rodney Andrew listened to my hard-luck tale, and I could tell he'd noticed that my suit jacket did not match the trousers. But he offered me job as a sub-editor at £18 a week. I jumped at it. As we shook hands he said: "By the way, if you are looking for accommodation, we have a flat you can have for £2 a week."

Saved.

I was still living at Michael's old home in Cosham, but early in November I got a call from Robina and went over to Catherington to stay with her until the new baby was due. Later that day, a Saturday, she announced that the time had come. Paw and I took her to the nursing home, reluctantly handed her over to the staff, and went back. Maw was busy amusing Yolanda. Paw and I sat up late over the kitchen stove, not talking much, until well after midnight.

The phone rang Sunday morning as I was drinking my morning tea: Robina was in labour – I should come at once. I handed Yolanda over to Maw and roared off on my bike the six or seven miles to Liss.

In the front hall, I was confronted by the sight of a young doctor charging downstairs. I grabbed his arm.

"There's an ambulance on the way," he said, "Don't worry. She's all right." Before I could ask, he rushed back upstairs. Something Robina had once told me snapped into my mind. Matron had impressed on her trainee nurses: "Walk. Don't run. A good nurse runs only in case of bleeding."

Most of my life passed before my eyes as I tramped up and down that hallway, yet I cannot recall any detail of the place. When the ambulance arrived, the young doctor, assisted by a couple of nurses, carried a ghostly Robina on a stretcher out to the waiting crew. She looked even more pale than I did, but she opened her eyes briefly and tried to smile as I sat beside her stretcher in the ambulance. A young nurse placed a little bundle beside her:

"Your new daughter," she said.

It was about 18 miles from Liss to St Mary's Hospital in Portsmouth, but it could have been 200 for all I knew. It was certainly the longest ride I'd ever known. Robina lay pale and sweating while the midwife mopped her forehead. Alongside, the mummy in its wrapping revealed a screwed-up face and a flattened, sloping head.

"Baby's fine," the midwife whispered. "She was the wrong way round, so the delivery was difficult, but she'll be perfectly all right. They are very determined little things, y'know."

I held Robina's hand and she gave me a slow smile again, then drifted off to sleep.

"Ah, please Lord, don't let me lose her...." I prayed over and over again. I couldn't have felt more guilty if I'd murdered my mother. Somehow I found I was holding the midwife's hand. Her lips moved and I realised she was praying, too.

"Where are you from?" I whispered.

"Stornaway – in the Hebrides."

"Highland and Islands," I told her. "Robina's family come from Oban. She's a Ness, from her father."

"Good omen," the girl said, smiling for the first time.

At the hospital I kept well clear until they'd carried Robina and our baby inside. After a couple of nervous hours, I was called to go up to the maternity wing. There was Robina, almost human, hair brushed, great green eyes shining. I kissed her and she pointed to the tiny, screwed-up but somehow self-satisfied little face alongside her.

"I love her already," I whispered. " We've already travelled a long way together."

"What shall we call her?" Robina said.

I suggested: "Something very appropriate?"

"Then, as today is Remembrance Sunday, let's call her Rosemary. You know, Shakespeare?"

"Rosemary – that's for remembrance."